Dear Shari

STEPPING STONES *to a*

Healthy Stepfamily

Blessings on the Journey!

Janet Nicholas, LPC LCDC EAP

Editorial Collaboration with Stacey Eskelin

Janet Nicholas

2017
Deviations, Inc.
Magnolia, Texas

Copyright 2017 by Janet Nicholas

Deviations, Inc.

Janet Nicholas, LPC LCDC EAP

26113 Oakridge Dr. Suite C

The Woodlands TX 77380

www.healthystepfamily.com

www.janetnicholas.com

Speaking Inquiries to

janet@healthystepfamily.com

978-0-9987435-0-9	Perfect bound book
978-0-9987435-1-6	MOBI ebook file
978-0-9987435-2-3	ePub ebook file

Book Packager and Project Coordinator — Rita Mills

www.3rdCoastBooks.com

Editors — Dimples Kellogg

Terri Looney

Stacey Eskelin

Faye Walker

Photos — J.D. Waterhouse Photography

Cover Design — Ken Fraser

The paper used in this publication meets the requirements of the American National Standard for Permanence of Paper for Printed Library Materials Z39.48-1984.

Printed in the United States of America

Dedication

*The Ultimate Guide in my life.
Thank you for being faithful and merciful, and always being
a lamp to my feet and a light to my path.*

*My amazing husband and partner. You are a gift from God. I
am so grateful to be on this journey with you.*

*My incredible children and grandchildren. My life would not
be the same without each of you.*

Table of Contents

Foreword

—◦—

There was no information on stepfamilies when I married my second husband in 1983. Like most stepfamilies, we started out with so much hope and excitement for our future. Here we'd beaten what seemed like insurmountable odds and found each other. We'd not only been given a fresh start, but a chance to get it right.

Like so many stepfamilies, we had no idea of the hardships that lay ahead, the potent psychological stew of subconscious expectations, personality conflicts, old marital wounds and emotional baggage that dated as far back as childhood. No one goes into a relationship with a "clean slate." But that slate becomes particularly colorful when attempting to merge families.

In the beginning, for every victory my husband and I experienced as a couple, as parents and now as stepparents, there were just as many defeats. At times, we wondered if we were going to make it. When John and Emily Visher, founders of the Stepfamily Association of America came to town in 1984, my husband and I headed to their lecture. Hearing their story was a ray of hope in our first year of marriage.

Even more daunting, I was studying to become a professional counselor during that period. I had a wealth of information, tools and insights to help with the unique challenges of stepfamilies. Yet, all of these tools were blunted in my hands—blunted by near-daily reminders of how far we had yet to go.

Education is so important, but equally important is experience, I realized. When I let go and let life teach me what I needed to know as a remarried stepparent, it all started coming together for me. I still used my "tricks of the trade," but I learned to combine them with instinct, patience, and eventually, love.

This is why working with stepfamilies has always been near and dear to my heart. I've been there. I lived it. My purpose then in writing this book is to give readers a realistic set of expectations, while at the same time instilling a sense of direction and hope. I want to also provide a viable roadmap to professionals working with stepfamilies.

As I began lecturing on this subject in 2009, I realized that the word "blend" (in relation to stepfamilies) fostered unrealistic expectations.

Stepfamilies don't really blend.

Instead, they merge over time; which is something that appeared to come as a huge relief to people attending my lectures who no doubt thought that they'd been doing something wrong. Weren't things supposed to be better at this point? Was this stepfamily business easier for other people than it was for them?

The bottom line is this: stepfamilies are on a journey. At first, the path looks easy. But once you venture down it, you start to notice the uphill climb.

In the early part of the journey, most stepfamilies stumble. But something happens if a family decides to stay the course. The path, while often rocky, grows more familiar. What a relief that is!

It then becomes the kind of journey that doesn't wear you down, but makes you stronger. Hardship forces you to grow.

Like any merger, it takes time for everyone to settle into new roles. Some never do. Family members can change birth order in one day. The youngest may now be the oldest. The oldest may now have more siblings to contend with. But adult stepfamilies can have just as many challenges as their younger counterparts. And often, no one sees them coming.

My goal then is to provide a pathway and to light a candle in what, for some, can appear to be considerable gloom. I do not do this alone. Of invaluable assistance were the researchers who have also been studying stepfamilies with great fervor : Dr. James Bray, Dr. Patricia Papernow, Dr. Judith Wallerstein, Drs. John and Emily Visher, Dr. Eileen Mavis Hetherington, Dr. Scott Browning, Dr. Kay Pasley and Dr. Francesca Adler-Baeder.

These are only a few people who have made an impact on stepfamily research. You will see more resources at the end of the book.

I also want to thank others who have walked this path with me: first and foremost is the Author and Finisher of my faith, my Rock and Refuge and my Ultimate Guide who has been diligent in showing me the next step each and every time.

Buddy Scott, my counselor, mentor and friend, and who it is no exaggeration to say, saved my life.

My mentor, Christine Scott, whose voice I still hear in my head even though she passed many years ago.

Rita Mills, my publisher and wonder woman, whose kind and gentle direction has made this project a reality.

My dear colleagues and friends, Paul Looney MD and Teri Looney. Their friendship and direction—not only with this book but in my life and the life I share with my dear husband, Scott, mean so much to me. Josie Pickett, who gave me direction and encouragement to finish this project.

Dimples Kellogg, who, as my first editor, encouraged me to publish this book.

To Stacey Eskelin, who apparently never sleeps. Her editing brought this work to life.

To my beautiful children and grandchildren. I am not the same without each and every one of you.

Last, but truly not least, to my wonderful husband, Scott, who brought me coffee when I needed it, talked me off the ledge on multiple occasions, and fixed my computer so many times, I've lost count.

Scott, you loved my child. I am so grateful to have you as my husband.

Here, then, are stories of stepfamilies and their journeys. All names and identifying information have been changed. Heartfelt thanks to those who were willing to share their challenges and their victories with me.

———•—•———

Introduction

⸺ ⸺

When I grew up in the 1950s, practically no one was divorced. The first time I heard that word was when my mother and grandmother were watching a soap opera called "As the World Turns" on our old black and white television set. Judging by the pained expressions on their faces and the hushed, dramatic tones of the soap opera actors when they uttered this scandalous new word, divorce, I stopped playing and paid attention. With the avid curiosity of a pre-kindergartener, I asked my mom what it meant. "It's when a husband and wife stop living together," she said.

I was puzzled. Alarmed. I asked her, "Would you and daddy ever get a divorce?" My parents fought bitterly. I never knew until that day that people could leave a marriage and the idea was terrifying to me.

Three years later, my parents sat me down and told me that one of our closest family members was getting a divorce. I cried and cried. It seemed like a fate worse than death, this sudden wrenching abandonment. I lived in fear that it could happen to me and watched anxiously when my parents fought. I felt that by paying attention, by being vigilant, I might pinpoint the exact moment when the tables finally tilted and divorce became the only viable solution to them.

My parents never did divorce. But years later, my worst fears played out in my own marriage. It was the 1980s by then, and it appeared as though practically everyone was divorcing. After a six-year marriage and with a baby in tow, my husband and I underwent all the agony and devastation of dissolving a union. It was something I was vehemently opposed to. My value system forbade it—you got married and stayed married. You worked things out, especially when there was a child involved. At church, I had silently judged the ones who were divorced, believing they should have done more to stay together. I lived in anger and misery, fearing that I was myself being judged. The most horrible fate in the world—that of single parenthood—awaited me now. All I could do was focus on raising my child to the best of my ability and hope to limit the emotional damage.

From our greatest pain often comes our greatest understanding. I sought the help I so clearly needed. I began my journey of healing with Buddy Scott at his loving and supportive counseling center. His mother, Christine, whose own marriage had culminated in divorce, was what I call a "thriving survivor." She mentored me, and together we developed a divorce recovery group.

Our numbers grew rapidly. It became apparent that divorced couples were facing new challenges—challenges that society really hadn't had to deal with before in quite the way that society was dealing with it now: the concept of stepparenting, remarriage, and families that have lost a spouse or a parent to death.

Eventually, I met an amazing man who was raising a child on his own. When we decided to marry, we promised each other that no matter what, we would make our marriage work. Both of us were concerned about the impact another divorce might have on our kids and were far from eager to recreate scenes from our previous marriages. A few years after tying what we hoped would prove to be a long sturdy knot, I returned to school, became a professional counselor and focused on stepfamilies as one of my areas of expertise.

After thirty-three years of being married to my wonderful husband and working with families that are struggling with the same complicated issues I was, I am surprised by how little information is out there on this most nuanced and weighty of subjects. It takes time for family members to get to know each other. A new family history must be painstakingly constructed, while at the same time memories of the previous marriage must be dealt with by children, teens, parents, exes, and even other family members.

What can you do when everyone wants this "second chance" to work out, but they're still dragging around pain, abandonment, and disappointment from the past? How do you ever learn how to trust again?

During my twenty-five years as a counselor, I have held a safe space for people who are navigating the rocky path of merging two families into one. I have heard many stories of loss, loneliness, abandonment, and divorce. And I have cheered many more on to victory. Suffering creates the opportunity to grow and to heal. We either learn from what has happened, or we try to ignore our pain and may become bitter or disillusioned.

Realizing there were few resources for my clients or for the public at large, I created a program called *Stepping Stones to a Healthy Stepfamily*—first as a seminar in 2009 and now as a book. Each time I presented the information, people urged me to write a book. The book was in the process, but a formal announcement of the book's title was made public at the Family Life Stepfamily Conference in Dallas, Texas, in 2013. This program to recovery is based on my experiences as a counselor, but also my journey as a daughter, mother, wife, stepmother, and grandmother.

Early on in my career, instead of my academic credentials, I used the initials given to me by my wonderful friend and counselor, Buddy Scott. He was the one who suggested I append I.B.T. to my name, which stood for I've Been There.

And I have.

As we start on this stepfamily journey, I want to share some good news! For years now research has stated the divorce rate in first marriages is fifty percent, second marriages, sixty percent, and third marriages even higher. The latest research by Shaunti Feldhahn, an eight-year exhaustive study of those original statistics, revealed this: The divorce rate for first marriages is approximately twenty to twenty-five percent, for second and third marriages, closer to thirty-one percent. For those of us re-marrieds, approximately sixty-eight to seventy percent stay married. That is good news, for certain! When I share this with stepcouples in my office, their faces exude a ray of hope, in spite of the challenges they are experiencing.

No matter what you may be going through as a divorced, widowed, or single parent—or as a newly remarried parent full of anxiety about the future or as someone who has been married for years—I can help you understand that no, you aren't crazy (although it feels that way sometimes), and you are not alone. Millions of families the world over are experiencing the exact same challenges you are going through right now. My avowed goal is to give you a proper set of tools, enabling you to identify what went wrong, how to talk about it, and what to do to fix it. I also hope this book will help you to see the things you're doing well.

You are not powerless. In fact, you are at the summit of your own wisdom, ready to take intelligent action. You started by asking questions and by picking up this book.

Everything you're going through is part of your life journey.

With this book, I'm going to see what I can do to help.

———————

STEPPING
STONES *to a*
Healthy Stepfamily

Stepping Stones
for Grief and Loss

The reality is that you will grieve forever. You will not 'get over' the loss of a loved one; you will learn to live with it. You will heal and you will rebuild yourself around the loss you have suffered. You will be whole again, but you will never be the same. Nor should you be the same nor would you want to.

—Elisabeth Kübler-Ross

As a therapist working with stepfamilies, one of the issues I help them talk about and consequently deal with are grief and loss from the past.

Grief is a journey. It is, perhaps, a journey that no one willingly embarks upon. Why would they? Pain, regret, and sorrow are gut-wrenching.

But what do they have to do with stepfamilies?

When a couple marries after the death, divorce, or ending of a relationship, there is newfound hope and excitement for a second chance. Some long for another incredible marriage, like they had with their deceased spouse. Those who divorced are longing for an opportunity to learn from their past and do it better. While the adults are dating, and feeling all the love and acceptance of this new relationship, the children most often view it with concern and the finality that their parents may not reconcile. Some children are reminded, "My parent has died and is not coming back." This can happen even with children who are happy about their parent's remarriage. As the stepfamily enters the journey ahead of them, inevitably, the past creeps back in. The far past of our family of origin and the more recent past of previous relationships and marriages. What is not dealt with will eventually resurface.

Let me start by saying that in order to build a solid foundation for the future, one needs to build a solid foundation from the past. If a person or family has unresolved grief, it needs to be dealt with. Otherwise, no solid foundation can be built, and no deep healing, understanding, or conflict resolution (if there is conflict) can be accomplished.

> Those emotions are muted simply because children don't have the vocabulary to express what they're feeling.

Adults and children can get stuck in any one of these grief stages when a family falls apart. Everyone wants to "move on" and forget about it. But some people stay angry for years, fueled by ongoing conflict or issues around having to pay child support or not receiving enough of it.

Other people are dealing with fallout over the death of a spouse—real world problems that now affect the living—unresolved anger from the first marriage, money issues because the deceased had been a poor manager of it and now the ones left behind must suffer for those mistakes. Or they could be grieving the loss of an amazing spouse and are now wondering how they could ever find someone that special again.

Children who are missing their deceased parent or divorced parent, who are grieving what they will never have again, don't always know they are grieving. Those emotions are muted simply because children don't have the vocabulary to express what they're feeling.

Yet there are others who, due to mental illness, depression, or anxiety get mired in the quicksand of sadness and need help getting out again.

The key is to give yourself permission to keep sorting through what works, what doesn't work, or what you thought was working but really isn't anymore. Grief has its own journey, and that journey is full of many different paths, all of which will bring you from the past to the present.

Grief has its own journey, and that journey is full of many different paths, all of which will bring you from the past to the present.

Our single biggest impediment to finding resolution and happiness is most of us will do anything to avoid pain. We wonder, often despairingly, how long it will take before we feel better. How long must we suffer through the heartache, the self-doubt, the eternal questioning of ourselves and others? Worse are the dark nights of the soul when we see for the first time the ways in which we may have contributed to our problems.

Some people are better than others at coping mechanisms like avoidance. Modern living has devised a thousand ways to do this—drugs and alcohol are two of the more obvious avoidance behaviors, but then there are the less "shameful" ones, such as excessive TV and Internet use, workaholism, even exercise. By employing these and other methods of stepping around grief and loss, a person can experience a false sense of resolution, only to have that grief resurface later on in life.

One of the most poignant instances of what can happen when a well-intentioned stepfamily tries to reconcile grief and loss from the past came up during a counseling session a few years ago.

The husband, Paul, had two girls from a previous marriage—Mallory, who was thirteen, and Alyson, who was eleven. He and his new wife, Felicia, had a toddler together; a rambunctious and adorable three-year-old named Max.

Paul exercised all his visitation, which meant Mallory and Alyson stayed with him and Felicia two weekends a month, six weeks over the summer, and alternating Christmases. The holiday visitation schedule had been informally amended by Paul and his ex-wife who, while not on the warmest terms, were at least civil. Mallory and Alyson spent Christmas morning with the ex-wife and then Christmas afternoon with Paul and Felicia.

But that's when the explosive emotional outbursts began.

Felicia, a pretty and vivacious woman who worked part-time as a buyer for a chain of department stores, grew up in Wichita, the child of two alcoholic parents. Christmases were usually spent with what she described as "earplugs and TV dinners." The TV dinners were because neither one of her parents had the emotional resources to put together a holiday dinner. The earplugs were there to deafen the sound of their constant fighting.

Like many children of alcoholics, Felicia vowed to give the children she would have one day the kind of beautiful, magical, fun-filled holiday she never enjoyed as a girl. We do that as parents, don't we? We have big pothole-sized wounds from our childhoods we attempt to fill as adults, even if what we're doing means absolutely nothing to the people we're doing it for. It's our way of "making things right again," only those wounds never do seem to heal up that well, do they? At least not by trying to use other people to fix what's wrong with us.

Their third Christmas as a family, Felicia went out of her way to decorate the house, play Christmas carols, bake holiday cookies, and wrap presents that were both thoughtful and expensive. Presents for everybody, but especially her two stepdaughters for whom she'd gone the extra mile to make feel welcome. "We seemed to get along okay," Felicia explained in my office, "but we weren't close. I wanted us to be, and I tried hard to bridge that gap. Maybe too hard." She frowned when she thought about it, and Paul reached over to squeeze her hand. "It didn't help that the girls never really gave me a chance."

Paul nodded. "They're at a difficult age," he admitted. "When they come over, it feels as though I'm losing them somehow, like they'd rather stay with their mom because all their friends live in her neighborhood. Dad just isn't that important anymore."

According to their new tradition, the girls spent the morning with their mom, Sara Jo, opening presents and eating a big holiday brunch. Like a lot of newly divorced, previously stay-at-home moms, Sara Jo was struggling to make up for lost ground in the work force. Much of her child support money had gone to buy presents.

"When it comes to the holidays, Sara Jo always feels ashamed and probably a little competitive," Paul explained. "She made the girls feel guilty about coming over, and she did that by talking about all the Christmases we had as a family before the divorce. The minute Mallory and Alyson walked into the house this year, I could tell they didn't want to be there. I could tell they resented being away from their mom, who was alone on Christmas, and they probably would have also liked being closer to their friends."

At thirteen, Mallory was naturally a little sullen. This would likely have been the case whether her parents were divorced or not. She sat on the couch and didn't say much, almost daring Felicia and her dad to try to make her enjoy anything. The younger daughter, Alyson, went straight to her room. Paul's attempts to get her to come out were in vain.

"I felt doubly hurt," Felicia explained. "First, because the girls were behaving like brats, but also because Paul wouldn't do anything to correct their behavior. I'd killed myself making Christmas beautiful and special for everybody, but no one appreciated what I'd done."

Paul had no wish to play the bad guy. He already felt as though his hold on the girls was slipping and he was no longer the most important man in their lives. At thirteen and eleven, his daughters were at a fairly unmanageable age to begin with. "I probably didn't discipline them as firmly as I should," Paul admitted. "I know Felicia was really upset about it. She started crying and ran to the bedroom. Mallory barricaded herself in her room, so it was just Max and me alone playing Thomas the Tank Engine. I felt like a total failure as a dad and as a husband."

The Christmas Day that Felicia had planned for, worked for, and looked forward to had officially turned into a holiday horror story—an all-too-common one, I'm afraid. In my counseling practice and in my own experience as a remarried parent, I understand and empathize with the pain and distress of all members of the family, including the ex-wife. And there is no more effective way for bringing volatile emotions to the surface than a high-expectation holiday like Christmas.

For early-journey stepfamilies, Christmas can be a minefield. There are all those memories of happier times to deal with—and not even happier times, necessarily, but at least times involving the original family. In the case of Paul and Felicia, Paul's guilt at having divorced his daughter's mother, combined with his fear of losing his daughters, made for a particularly distressing situation.

Felicia, a self-described romantic idealistic, had issues of her own to face long before her perfect Christmas went bust. She felt defensive about her position in the family and fearful of what might happen if Paul's daughters turned against her. Would Paul abandon her, too? How would she learn to deal with her resentment when Paul gave into the demands of his teenage daughters without regard for her own needs and wishes?

Unspoken here, too, I soon realized, was the terrible grief and loss Paul's daughters were suffering, especially Mallory. As the older daughter, she remembered two more intact family Christmases than Alyson did. She remembered the cozy get-togethers with cousins and aunts and grandparents, the tree with silver heirloom ornaments, the family tradition of going out together to look at all the holiday lights in the neighborhood.

Now, her mother worked all the time and still had trouble making ends meet. When her mother got home after a long day and even longer commute, she didn't have a lot of energy left over for her daughters.

And this is at the crux of why there are so many problems in stepfamilies and why parents often don't get it. They don't always understand that children and teens grieve so differently. Sometimes a child's behavior looks regressive (or aggressive), when all they're doing is grieving. Some unexpressed and powerful emotion has hit them at their core, only they don't have a clue about how to deal with it or even what is going on inside of themselves.

Paul and Felicia and their family did get through this, and things did get better. But Mallory's sense of loss was complete when her father remarried. Here he had this great new life with his second wife and had started a new family. Even though Mallory and Alyson lived with their mother, she was no longer available to them in the same way she had been before the divorce. Add a healthy, normal dose of teenage angst, and it was little wonder everything seemed as though it were flying apart.

The Six Stages of Healing

Elisabeth Kübler-Ross, a Swiss-American psychiatrist and pioneer in near-death studies, chronicled her work with terminally ill patients in 1969 in her groundbreaking book, On Death and Dying. Based on years of extensive research, she discovered there were five distinct stages people went through after loss. Those stages are:

- Shock
- Denial
- Anger
- Bargaining
- Acceptance

These stages do not progress in any particular order. They can happen over a few seconds or a period of years. Typically, it takes about two years for a person to properly grieve a major loss like death or divorce. For many people, the grieving process moves at a snail's pace because they don't allow themselves the "luxury" of inconvenient emotions. They never fully recover because they never fully inhabit the place in their own hearts where grief continues to live.

During the initial stage of grieving, people experience a state of shock and denial so powerful they cannot and will not believe their loss is occurring. Shock is the mind's way of giving us a psychological buffer until we are better prepared to deal with the gravity of our situation. When problems occur, it is usually when a client becomes stuck in these first and second stages of shock and denial and has trouble moving past them; however, the possibility of stalling out in any one of these grief stages is always there.

In American society, in particular, men find themselves unwilling, or perhaps, unable to express sadness. Women, too, can be afraid to let themselves go for fear of the effect they think it will have on their children. But sadness is a normal emotion, and it is healthy for children to observe a parent being sad.

It goes without saying that exhibiting sadness around your children must be done wisely and maturely. Some parents try to turn their children into tiny counselors, insisting they listen to things that are way above their emotional paygrade. Or they express grief as a means of manipulating their children into telling the other parent how much mommy or daddy is crying and upset.

Other parents do the exact opposite. They show zero emotion except a brittle, artificial happiness, which is terribly confusing for children who can sense otherwise.

Parents are the emotional standard bearers. Your children learn how to react in healthy (or unhealthy) ways based on the behavior you model for them. Of course, children also need to be reassured everything will be okay, but it is a mistake to think we must do all of our grieving out of their view unless we sense grieving has an ulterior motive.

This must be done in a balanced way. We cannot use our children as surrogate spouses, and we cannot rely on them to help us sort through our grief. They will have their own work to do.

All too often in stepfamilies, anger, which is the third stage of grief, is met with more of the same. Stressed, angry parents—when confronted with stressed, angry children—respond in kind, which feeds a never-ending loop of hurt, angry feelings. We are very quick to blame people or circumstances for our emotional states. In a way, this prevents us from feeling empowered enough to take responsibility for our own emotional wellbeing. Some people get caught up in a pattern of self-blame. Should have, could have, would have, may become frequent phrases in their heads.

Yet, anger must be welcomed just like any other emotion. Why? Because anger turned inward may lead to depression. Turned outward—and channeled in a healthy way—it can become energy. Healthy anger can help us to grow, to return to school, to face the challenges ahead, and, perhaps, one day to even find the humor in our situation. Left unresolved, however, it can lead to bitterness and possible inertia.

As a therapist, I have seen firsthand the galvanizing effects of anger.

Women are often the ones who have the hardest time expressing it. Most men have less trouble being angry, in large part because society sanctions the behavior in men—anger is okay, but sadness isn't. When you're a "real" man, you can be angry. It makes you appear strong and invulnerable, but it sometimes doesn't leave a lot of room to be human.

Unfortunately, women are not conditioned to vent in the same way. For them, anger is a much scarier proposition and receives far less support from family in particular or society at large.

Beneath anger, of course, for both men and women, is fear. Getting to the root of fear is what matters, and the sooner we can identify the source of that fear, the better.

In the bargaining stage, it is customary to blame yourself for everything that went wrong. However, we can also blame others, such as our former spouse. Children, with their magical thinking, are especially prone to self-blame What if I'd taken out the trash when mom asked me to? Maybe she and dad wouldn't have argued about it and then they wouldn't have broken up. What if I'd gotten better grades or not fought so much with my sister?

But kids don't have a monopoly on "if only." What parent hasn't been eaten up with guilt over some imagined negligence on their part? If only they'd arrived five minutes earlier, their child wouldn't have gotten hurt. Maybe if they hadn't spent night after night recovering from work in front of the TV, they might have seen what was happening inside their own family.

Many people—believers and non-believers both—start bargaining with a higher power.

1. Take me, not them.

2. God, please fix this situation for me and I promise to stop drinking so much.

3. If we hadn't gotten a divorce, our children would be doing better in school.

4. Surely, if I just tried harder and lost weight, I'd feel better about myself, and then this pain of rejection wouldn't sting so much.

5. Maybe if I'd focused on my family instead of my career, I wouldn't have lost everything that mattered to me.

6. If only he/she would have tried harder.

7. Why didn't my ex see what was happening before it was too late?

8. We could have gone to counseling, but we didn't.

Most of the time, guilt and shame and endless what ifs force our attention on the past and prevent us from focusing on what we can do about our situation right this minute. However, it is a necessary and normal part of the grief journey.

The last of Elisabeth Kübler-Ross's five stages of grief is acceptance. This stage leads us to the realization that yes, some awful thing has happened, and no, we cannot change it.

Acceptance allows us to come to terms with the inevitable. It ushers us out of shock and denial and into the true reality of the situation so we can deal with it. Painful though it may be, acceptance paves a way for us to cope with loss.

I would like to add a sixth stage to this emotional arc—Forgiveness. C.S. Lewis says,

"Everyone says forgiveness is a lovely idea until they have something to forgive." It is so much easier said than done. But here are some important facts about forgiveness:

1. Forgiveness isn't an emotion. It's a choice.

2. Forgiveness is not forgetting.

3. Forgiveness is for the forgiver, so you can move forward.

4. Forgiveness grows over time.

5. Forgiveness is not trusting again—although there are times when some trust or even full trust can be restored. For some this is not possible—and could even be dangerous.

6. You will continue to sort and grieve through the stages. Each time you do, you can grow and deepen into your forgiveness.

7. When a loss or wound is grieved to completion, the feelings associated with forgiveness show up: serenity and peace. We can experience healing.

In some situations, there is no need for forgiveness because no one is responsible for the loss. But in other situations, we may harbor toxic amounts of anger and resentment, even toward ourselves.

In most marriages that end in divorce, there are usually a host of unresolved issues with the ex-spouse. Giving yourself permission to revisit those past hurts and wounds is to ensure you move quicker through your grief.

Even in situations where there was a death of a spouse, unresolved issues can be shelved out of a sense of guilt or disloyalty.

So how can understanding these six stages of grief help you fix what might be wrong with your current situation? How will it guide you through the grieving process and lead you to place of happiness and strength on your journey?

Even traditional families are rife with real and perceived wrongs, bristling with resentments and grief. Imagine then the extraordinary stressors at work within a stepfamily.

Sometimes it feels as though every single member of that family is speaking a different language. The truth is, they are.

Sometimes it feels as though every single member of that family is speaking a different language. The truth is, they are. We bring our baggage with us. The weight of that baggage can be crippling.

Even during happy times, a mature stepfamily of many years can be reminded of loss or hopes which never materialized. It's not bad or wrong; it just is. As always, how we manage those feelings is what matters.

———•◦•———

Grief Management Stepping Stone

One method of grieving I created for my clients is what I call "grief management." Some losses are so disturbing and powerful we succumb to grief cycles, and they appear to have no end in sight.

Here is one method that will help. It gives us a healthy way to address those feelings safely and without extreme immersion or avoidance.

- Find a separate notebook or journal for this grief work. Also, find a box with a lid. We'll call this your "grief box." It's where you will store your journal and anything else which reminds you of that person or situation, such as photos, jewelry, or mementos from a special occasion. You only need a few items. The purpose is to stir up your feelings of grief. But you are choosing the time and the place.

- Be sure to keep your journal inside the box and out of sight so your privacy will be respected, but also so you can avoid seeing it every time you walk into that space in your home.

- Each morning, if at all possible, get up before everyone else and set a timer for fifteen minutes.

Go to a private place, and get your journal and all the items out of the box.

Typically, as you look at the items, feelings will begin to surface. Write in your journal without worrying about punctuation or grammar. You may begin by writing five feeling words such as angry, sad, worried, overwhelmed, disappointed, and resistant. If you are not good about identifying how you feel, use the list of feeling words in the appendix and keep the list inside your journal. You can actually grow your "feeling vocabulary."

———————

You may want to write a letter to the person(s) associated with the loss. You will not ever send these letters; they are for you. Writing and mailing a letter to another person changes the tone of the letter. We tend to hold back or let loose rather than deal with what is going on inside us. Some of my faith-based clients write letters to God. This can be strange for agnostics and atheists, but even for non-believers, there can be feelings of anger at life or the universe or whatever supreme intelligence they call on in times of distress. Yet, writing to God in whatever way one conceives of God to be is wonderfully cathartic.

- If tears come up, let them. If shock or denial or anger come up, let them. Pour it all out on paper. When the timer goes off, stop. Don't judge what you have said or done. Then place your journal and items back in the grief box and put them away. You can say a prayer over your work. You can also make a statement such as, "I have done all I can do this morning. Now I will move forward with my day."

- If you have written anything in your journal you would not want someone to find, tear that page out and shred it, signifying you are letting go of this piece of your grief. Some have buried or burned their writings in a cathartic ritual that helps them get rid of that part of their grief.

As the day goes on, you may notice—especially in the early stages of grief—that those feelings will resurface at the least convenient times. But you don't have to let yourself be owned by them. You have a choice. If possible, stay focused on your day. Reassure yourself, "I will make sure to have another grief session tonight, but for now I need to stay focused."

My clients and I have found in our grief process if we jump-start our day with grief management and repeat this process in the evening before bed, we slowly gain a better handle on our grief. In the evening, set the time for fifteen or twenty minutes and repeat the process from earlier that morning. Within seven to fourteen days, most people find the grief to be significantly lessened.

As difficult as it is to take any form of action, especially when you're frozen inside and barely coping, writing out what you're feeling is a step in the right direction. Clients who have committed to the morning and evening grief management sessions have found the grief does not own them anymore.

Plenty of clients in the past have argued they don't like doing the work in the morning. "I wake up feeling terrific," they say. Or, "I'm too exhausted to feel anything in the morning." But in the early grief period, especially, it is important to do the work, however impossible it

> **Loss is not a straight line. It is more of a path with many twists and turns. If you pay attention to your grief, the path gets easier.**

may seem. If we don't face our demons, they will creep up on us slowly during the day and ambush us when we least expect it.

Loss is not a straight line. It is more of a path with many twists and turns. If you pay attention to your grief, the path gets easier.

For every "good" day you have, there will be two or three more devastating days. Sometimes you'll be really clicking along, congratulating yourself even on how well you're doing, and then bam! It will feel as though you're back to square one again, in shock or denial, feeling angry or sad, questioning your forgiveness.

But as you address your stages of grief, the need for grief management sessions will recede. Pretty soon you start having far more pain-free days than pain-filled ones. Many people find after a while, they don't need regular grief sessions anymore. Every so often, they'll pull out their grief journal and do some work in it.

Increasingly, the journal itself becomes a time capsule, a powerful reminder of where they were once but are no longer. It becomes a silent witness to everything they've survived, everything that has made them a thousand times stronger and more compassionate as a person.

Questions for the Journey

1. Have there been disappointments or losses you have not dealt with in your stepfamily?

2. Were there disappointments prior to your remarriage, your previous marriage, or your life prior to those events?

3. Did you have specific hopes and expectations prior to this marriage?

4. If so, how have you dealt with the hopes and expectations that have not been realized?

5. What losses or changes have your children or teens had to face? A move to new resident? New school? New siblings? Change in birth order with new stepfamily?

6. How often do you allow them to talk about these losses and changes with you without interrupting, justifying, or explaining your position?

7. If you are currently experiencing feelings of loss, where are you in the grief process?

Stepping Stones for Dealing with Emotional Baggage

*Every major difficulty you face in life is a fork in the
road. You choose which track you will head down, toward
breakdown or break through.*

—John C. Maxwell

We all have baggage. Some of it is positive and healthy
things we need to keep. Some of our baggage, well, not
so much.

Our bags contain leftovers, which are emotions from the past that we
stuff away and forget about.

Unfortunately, we have to deal with those issues sooner or
later, and quite often the life events that are the hardest, the ones that
bring us to our knees, are the exact moments when they begin to spill
out, appearing again in all their glory.

My baggage centered around the issues of money and control.
My parents were loving, blue-collar, hardworking people. Money
was not plentiful when I was growing up, but my folks made sure I

had the things which were important to me, such as art lessons and horses. Still, there were tensions, fears and anxieties—and I absorbed them all.

Yet after my divorce, as is true of many single mothers, money became extremely tight. My old fears about not having enough money sucker-punched me. Without a degree at that time, I had limited opportunities for advancement in the large company where I worked. Twelve thousand dollars a year wasn't much to live on by any standard, let alone trying to raise and feed a child on that small amount.

There were times when unforeseen crises—the car breaking down, my child getting sick—ate up my entire paycheck, leaving me destitute until the next pay period, which always seemed to be two weeks away.

In the 1980s, getting a credit card in your own name after a divorce was next to impossible. I was terrified of what might happen and spent a great deal of time trying to control myself, my job, and my surroundings.

The terror of not having enough money pursued me every waking minute and even in nightmares. All those old messages I had received as a child by my well-intentioned parents came flooding back. They were messages about fear and scarcity.

It took me quite a while to overcome my emotional "leftovers" about money, but with hard work, I made it past those obstacles, and was able to eventually put money into a savings account in case of emergency.

Yet when I remarried and became a stay-at-home mom, every single one of those fears about not having enough money returned, and they brought along friends.

For starters, I felt vulnerable about not having a job and not bringing home a paycheck. What if my new husband left or died? My response to this was to double down on controlling the people and the things around me. Even going to the grocery store brought me so much anxiety, I could barely make it through the checkout line without experiencing a panic attack.

I realized this leftover was getting the best of me. Despite my reluctance to admit I was terrified and vulnerable and decidedly not in control, I finally shared my distress with my husband. He and I came up with a budget that made me feel more secure.

With time, something as innocuous as going to the grocery store returned to being a mundane event rather than an event filled with sweating and heart palpitations. I realized obsessing about what I could not control was exhausting and useless, and I learned to relax at a deeper level into my new marriage.

Sorting through our unhealthy baggage and dumping out what no longer works in our new relationship is vital. Carrying around all that extra stuff makes the journey more difficult.

Sorting through our unhealthy baggage and dumping out what no longer works in our new relationship is vital.

Money and control may seem like obvious baggage. However subtle, they have the power to impact a stepfamily in its formative stages or even many years down the line.

On average, it takes five to seven years to become a relatively established stepfamily. Five to seven years. Understanding what is going on inside the hearts and minds of all members of your family is essential. Everyone is on a different timetable. Every stepfamily has its own extenuating circumstances—how well do the remarried spouses get along with their exes? What are the ages of the children involved?

Sometimes you have no other option than to patiently respect the processes of grieving, rejecting, and reconciliation.

On average, it takes five to seven years to become a relatively established stepfamily.

Yet most experts agree it is the first two years of a remarriage which are the most challenging—the first year especially. Understanding what might be going on will help you bring necessary peace to your stepfamily.

Here are a few of the stepping stones to help you along your journey.

———•+•———

Ties that Bind — What to Look for in Stepfamily Attachment

One of the most important things to remember when assimilating people into a new stepfamily is it does not become a merged family without memories of past attachments. It is important to remember stepfamilies are created out of loss—divorce, death, or a relationship where the parents never married.

Loyalty to the biological parent, whether that parent is alive or deceased, may make it difficult for any child to accept a remarriage.

Researcher Dr. Judith Wallerstein in her brilliantly researched book, The Unexpected Legacy of Divorce: A Twenty-Five Year Landmark Study, identified some common reactions children may have. And I would like to touch on them here so you have a point of reference with your own family.

Girls at any age may fear losing their mother to a man. This is as common in young female children as it is in adult female children. The bond between a mother and a daughter is wholly unique. Many girls feel as though their mother's divided attention means less love for them.

Some boys may be grateful to have a man around the house. Having another male to watch football or bond with over shared chores (or shared "male" perspectives) can be a huge help. If the biological father is lacking in these areas, the opportunity to "learn how to be a man" is a welcome one. Some boys, however, may resent a male figure taking over his perceived place as "man of the house."

Dr. James Bray of Baylor College of Medicine conducted a nine-year study on stepfamilies that will help us gain an even deeper understanding of the dynamics involved.

Doing the legwork now to grasp what's at stake during a remarriage, especially for children, will save you a lot of stress further down the line. You will feel less bewildered when a child's "troubling" behavior first appears. That behavior can manifest as outbursts, withdrawal, acting out, or sadness at home or at school. You will be able to identify it for what it is—not a sign your new partnership is doomed to failure, but rather a cry for help from a child trying to understand what's going on.

In Dr. Bray's study, both the woman and man who were remarrying had children, although the man did not have primary custody of his biological children.

In any first marriage, there is usually a honeymoon period when the couple has time to focus exclusively on their relationship.

But when two families merge, the needs of the couple are immediately challenged by the needs of the children. This is partly what makes the first two years such an uphill journey.

Dr. Bray's study suggests four key tasks must be addressed within the first two years in order to facilitate a successful merging of the two families. I have found these tasks to be spot on in the stepfamilies I have worked with over the years.

1. Determining the role of the stepfather and his involvement in the lives of the woman's children.

2. Creating a satisfying second marriage and finding ways to distinguish it from the first marriage.

3. Managing change.

4. Creating rules that work for nonresidential parents and former spouses.

During years three through five, general harmony improved for stepfamilies—not just by modest margins, but by a whopping two hundred percent. By being given the time necessary to learn the quirks, habits, and endearing traits of one another, the new family managed to figure it out.

But just because things were better in the stepfamily didn't mean there weren't problems. If a child or teen was struggling with one or both parents, those issues could still create reverberations throughout the family and beyond. By this point, however, the family itself seemed better equipped to deal with them.

In Bray's study on years six through nine, there were some surprises.

He found those families that had children entering their teen years were, predictably, stressed during what is a notoriously difficult period for everyone. The teen years presented challenges for the stepfamily as a whole, but the couple suffered as well.

However, the roots on this new family tree had now grown sturdy enough to withstand the storm of adolescence. The parents had usually bonded as a couple, and because of that bond, they were better equipped to deal with whatever came their way.

Researcher Dr. Judith Wallerstein identified an adolescent's resurgence of grief around his parents' divorce as the "Sleeper Effect." This often takes parents by surprise, especially if the grief stems from something they considered a resolved situation.

In her book Second Chances, Dr. Wallerstein says, "Ours is the first report of the Sleeper Effect in children of divorce—it was simply not known to exist until we had the opportunity to follow these children for at least ten years after their parents separated. Because they were well-adjusted during adolescence and performed so well in high school, the troubles they are experiencing now at entry into young adulthood came as a complete surprise."

When the Sleeper Effect has been triggered, stepfamily couples find themselves fielding a lot of questions from their preteens or teens about the previous marriage. Timing-wise, this coincides with teens entering their own dating relationships, which causes some of them to become highly critical of their parents' marriages, both past and present, and often of the parents themselves.

Culture is also an important point of consideration when working with stepfamilies. There are significant cultural differences in stepfamilies depending on whether they are Latino, Asian, African-American, or Jewish, and whether the family has been in the United States for one or several generations. Also, there is racial diversity within couples themselves, which then translates into a different set of stepfamily issues—cultural growing pains as well as familial ones.

Also, with diversity in couples marrying today, so it is with stepfamilies.

Although research on this subject is scarce, what research we do have indicates Latinos in particular resist being labeled a stepfamily. To them, the concept of "family" is a fluid and inclusive one. Some Latinos are reluctant to even admit they are a stepfamily.

Research on African-American stepfamilies indicates, on the whole, these stepfamilies may progress more quickly. Some African-American stepfamilies I interviewed agreed with these findings, confirming African-Americans do tend to parent each other's children. This means friends, neighbors, grandparents, aunts, uncles, and even extended family will intervene when there are problems. When a stepparent enters the picture, it can be easier for them to integrate into the family because the family borders are already wonderfully porous.

However, a few African-American parents I interviewed said it took some time before their children accepted the new husband. Issues with their birth father were a constant source of pain and frustration, which made it tough for them to trust the new man in their lives. It took time and empathy and infinite patience, but now their children don't even think twice about it. They tell everyone they have two dads.

There is minimal research on Asian stepfamilies. Plus, there are many different cultures to consider—Chinese, Vietnamese, Korean,

Japanese. What we do know is stepfamilies are on the rise in Asian culture and they experience the same growing pains as everyone else.

———

The Unfinished Business of Emotional Baggage

This is my husband's story. I am including it because it illustrates how painful our unresolved issues can be, even as adults, and the positive impact that can happen when those issues are finally addressed.

Scott's parents divorced when he was about two years old, and both remarried soon after. His mother, who had custody of Scott, died in childbirth when he was four years old. His baby sister died as well.

For most of us, the ability to remember the past does not solidify until the age of five or thereabouts, and so it was for my husband. He had no memories of his mother, which filled him with a terrible sense of loneliness. He could look at the photos of her holding him before she died, but he had no specific recollections.

It is clear she loved him, which in a way made things harder. In all his photos, he was carefully dressed and lovingly groomed. She must have felt what many mothers feel: awe that such a perfect little human being had come from her.

However, after his mother's death, a nasty custody battle ensued. Scott's maternal grandparents decided they wanted to raise him. This left a great deal of animosity between Scott's newly remarried father and Scott's maternal grandparents.

Such a custody fight was rare in the 1950s, and his father and stepmother maintained their custody of him. But he was never told the details of his mother's life or of his parents' divorce. It left a significant gap in his understanding of himself, where he came from, and why his mother was never spoken of.

After the death of his maternal grandmother some years later when Scott was about fifty, a letter arrived from his mother's best friend. She had never forgotten Scott. He had often played alongside her own children. She told Scott that if he wanted to know more about his mother, she would send him reliable information.

He wrote, thanking her for the opportunity to know more about his mother, and his mother's friend replied with a beautiful, richly detailed letter about how much his mother had loved him. He was shocked to discover the life of his mother and infant sister had been cut tragically short because of the doctor's failure to diagnose gestational diabetes.

His mother had apparently beseeched her own mother to "Take care of Scotty." It was why his grandmother had given his father and stepmother so much trouble and had fought them so hard in court. She had made a promise to her dying daughter. Of course, she felt compelled to keep it. Until that moment, he had never understood her combative behavior. Now, it made perfect sense.

My husband, Scott, and I were dining out one night after his grandmother's funeral when he asked me, "Why do you think my stepmother never adopted me?"

I told him it was a great question and suggested he call her and ask. His stepmother told him she had always wanted to adopt him, but feared it would create further tensions between her and Scott's grandmother.

Scott promptly flew to his hometown, met with his parents and a judge, and became the oldest adoptee in that town's history!

So what are we to understand from all this? What's the takeaway, and how can we apply it to our own stepfamily situation?

———•+•———

Stepping Stones for the Journey

- Don't make the mistake of believing that just because your new family isn't facing challenges at the moment, all is well and will remain that way. Issues come up for different people at different times, but the one thing for certain is they will come up. Your best way to prepare is to take care of your issues first. Using the journaling technique outlined in Chapter One, you will be better able to vent any confusion, frustration, grief, loss, and anger about your previous marriage or your present one. Family of origin issues can also arise. Rip up or ceremonially shred any part of that journal that you feel might be read by someone else. Do everything you can to ensure your privacy so there is no temptation to hold back. Some of the best therapy you can get is the therapy you give yourself.

- Strike a balance between your feelings and your thoughts. If you feel threatened by your spouse's refusal to see how his inability to discipline his kids causes you to feel unloved, own it. This can originate from your past as well—how clearly you were or were not heard as a child in your family or in your previous marriage. Resist any temptation to manipulate the situation in your favor. You've got to be really direct about how other people's behavior makes you feel, but you mustn't fall prey to the idea that just because they know how their behavior affects you, they owe you something. Yes, O.P.B. (Other People's Behavior) can be hurtful; all too often we are operating on false assumptions about why they're doing it. We have maybe half the correct information and make up the rest in our heads. Nobody owes you their automatic obedience. Successful stepfamilies are successful because they have learned how to be understanding and flexible.

Leftovers are never easy, but they must be dealt with. Parents are required to do some serious "adulting," and that often means being patient when your patience is at an end and being diplomatic when you're fresh out of diplomacy. You will occasionally fail. Things will be said which you can't take back. Misfires will happen you will later regret. This, too, is part of stepfamilies. Be patient with people. Be patient with yourself, too.

―――――・◆・―――――

Questions for the Journey

Consider journaling about the following questions:

1. What leftovers do you think you may have from your family of origin? Your previous relationships? Your previous marriage?

2. What methods are you using to address your emotional baggage? Consider how you might build new skills to lighten your load.

3. Have you considered how your current spouse may have dealt with his or her leftovers?

4. What leftovers might be affecting your relationship with your children or stepchildren?

5. Consider what leftovers your children and stepchildren might be experiencing.

―――――・◆・―――――

Stepping Stones for Couples

Blessed are the flexible, for they shall not be bent out of shape.

—Buck Brannaman

If there is one thing I've consistently noticed over the years as a therapist, it is this: A family is only as strong and durable as the pair-bond of the couple.

In order to stay viable, a couple must find ways to connect—and traditional dating methods like dinner and a movie are often side-lined by the very real demands of making a living and raising kids.

For most stepfamily couples, there is never a honeymoon period. They go from single parents to remarried parents with no time for them to bond exclusively as a couple. They exchange one house for another house, only now the kids sometimes have other kids they are obligated to share things with. It takes a lot of flexibility to be a stepcouple.

There is stress, and that stress tends to accumulate. It doesn't help that two of those stressors can be intimacy and money, which can be two of the major causes of breakups. It's difficult to focus on each other in a meaningful way when there are kids in the house, and that holds true for both original families and remarried ones.

But with stepfamilies, there are unique stressors: the children's other parents, scheduling between two homes, different rules at different houses, child support, private or embarrassing information shared with the child's other parent, parenting differences, sibling and stepsibling rivalries. These are just a few issues traditional, first-time marriages don't experience.

All those slow, romantic Sunday mornings that childless couples have the luxury of enjoying just aren't possible when kids arrive. But at least first families have a chance to ease into parenthood. With stepfamilies, it can be more like a "just add water" and presto, change-o, instant family.

When the Pair Bond is Threatened

As a therapist, I worked with a family a few years ago, where Adele, the stepmother, a straight-shooting corporate attorney in her early forties had married Peter, a commercial developer with two children from a previous marriage. While they were dating, Adele and Peter had no trouble in their relationship. He had his kids every other weekend and Adele mostly did her own thing—antiquing, bike riding, yoga. But when they married, Adele found herself having to share her life, her house and her husband with two children, a boy of eight and a girl, eleven. Tensions quickly escalated.

For most stepfamily couples, there is never a honeymoon period.

"I never wanted kids," Adele would say. "I had no experience with them, so of course I had no way of knowing how difficult this would be—the whining, the fighting, the refusal to eat anything that wasn't a French fry or a chicken nugget. Even getting them to brush their teeth became a major ordeal. My mother never let me get away with behavior like that, so I guess it's hard to understand why Peter lets them do whatever they want when they're here. At least, that's what it feels like to me."

In both his first and now his second marriage, Peter had a very relaxed parenting style. "I'm not a helicopter dad," he said. "I believe in leading by example, not by force or demand. I don't get to see my kids as much as I would like to anyway. Why ruin what little time we have together with pointless arguing?"

Yet Adele continued to feel neglected. "Even on the weekends we spend together without the kids, Peter usually watches a game on TV. Sometimes he goes out golfing with his friends. So where does that leave me? I feel like I went from being the most important woman in his life to being wallpaper. It embarrasses me when I run into friends and they ask me why I'm never out with my husband. I end up having to over-explain my situation and the longer I talk, the worse it sounds."

Unfortunately, Peter was falling into his old habit of just relaxing on the weekend and had grown increasingly tone-deaf to the subtle and not-so-subtle hints dropped by his new wife about them spending time together. There didn't seem to be much flexibility on his part. Peter did what Peter wanted, which was perfectly valid, except that he'd added a wife into the equation. Wives require attention. Without intimacy and shared experiences to cement the relationship, there is no relationship.

This was clearly an emotional leftover for Peter. His mother required little of him growing up and enjoyed taking care of him until he left for college. In his first marriage, it wasn't long before this became a big problem, and here he was facing it again.

But Adele had a few issues of her own to deal with. When you marry a man with children, you aren't just marrying that man. By default, you are marrying his children, his parents, and his ex-wife, too. It's a package deal. And there are going to be times—plenty of them, in fact—when the only way you're going to survive all that is by re-membering what you liked about your husband in the first place.

Relationships function according to those principles. Love can sometimes feel like a mental abstraction, like something you think you feel more than you actually feel in any one particular moment. It can rattle people who aren't used to perceiving love this way. They tend to believe love is this ever-constant, never-varying thing.

> Love is a commitment, regardless of how you feel. It is the glue that helps when the going gets tough and you don't feel like loving someone.

Love is a commitment, regardless of how you feel. It is the glue that helps when the going gets tough and you don't feel like loving someone.

But that's precisely why mental health professionals like me are forever saying relationships require real effort. Sometimes you have to "fake it" until you feel it again. Sometimes you have to buckle down and make sacrifices of time, money, and comfort in order to do what's right by the family as a whole, not just one or two of its senior members.

Mistakes will be made on both sides. You can count on that. Nobody gets it right all the time.

How Our Ability to Bond Becomes Damaged

In the following true story, the mother of a client of mine experienced abandonment issues as a young girl. How it played out in her young life affected the kind of men she was drawn to.

My client, Kathy, a brisk, capable woman in her early fifties, said her parents divorced when she was about nine years old. Both her parents had been in ministry, and her father ran off with a coworker, which made things tough for his kids because everyone lived in the same small community.

At first, her father made an effort to visit. He sent presents. One day a package arrived containing expensive gifts of jewelry for each child.

Kathy was ecstatic, but her mother wasn't. Her mother was livid.

Kathy's mother got a hammer and ordered her kids to smash the jewelry. All of it. Kathy didn't want to. She was heartbroken about destroying such a lovely and thoughtful gift from a father she'd never stopped loving. But she did as she was told. Her mother then gathered the smashed pieces and put them into the box they were mailed in. She sent the box back to her ex-husband.

He never contacted them again.

Unfortunately, this kind of situation is far from rare. Such scenes may just as easily play out behind closed doors or in furious online exchanges. Consequently, some children may not ever know why their parent suddenly disappeared or slowly faded from their lives.

What proved to be so confusing for Kathy was she had no idea why her father abandoned her. This abandonment haunted her for the rest of her life—so much so, she tracked down where he lived, which turned out to be only a few hundred miles from her original hometown.

Kathy met him, his wife, and their child—her own half-sibling, flesh-and-blood she'd never even laid eyes on before. Then she asked her father point-blank, "Why didn't you come for me after I grew up and moved away from my mother?" Having raised children of her own, Kathy found his behavior incomprehensible. How did you not attempt to reunite with your own children, especially when they were no longer living with the one person who made it clear your presence wasn't wanted?

But when Kathy finally met her dad, he was already terminally ill and died a few months later.

She never got an answer to her question.

For Kathy, the emotional fallout from her childhood manifested itself in her adult life as a tendency to seek out men who were emotionally unavailable. How could you trust a flawed, unpredictable, slightly dangerous thing like a human being? It took us a while before she was able to nourish a real friendship and longer than that before she could date, but it eventually happened.

———•+•———

Dr. James Bray — The Three Different Types of Stepfamilies

Since understanding the stepfamily dynamic is important to the health of any couple, it pays to know the different types of stepfamilies and how they function.

Some people will identify their "style" immediately; others will see themselves as more of a combination. Yet familiarizing yourself with the three types of stepfamilies will help you feel less alone and less apt to believe there is nothing that can be done about the problems bedeviling your family right now.

Always remember knowledge is power.

Neotraditional

After several years, a neotraditional family will start to look like a first family. The stepfather proceeds slowly with his stepchildren and seems comfortable with the mother being the primary caregiver. Researchers observe that although this type of stepfamily appreciates help from former spouses and former in-laws, the couple has their challenges just like any other. When they see things are not working, they are willing to redirect their efforts to creatively problem solve. They perceive themselves as a family, but become more realistic about expectations, and patiently respect the fact children and teens need time to adjust. A lot of time. Grownups do, too.

Matriarchal

The second type of stepfamily researchers identified is the Matriarchal. A Matriarchal stepfamily has a strong, competent, take-charge kind of wife or mother. Usually, the husband is content to remain in the background, but there is never any doubt he is attracted to and appreciative of his wife's ability to manage things.

A typically Matriarchal husband is focused on the marriage, with parenting taking a secondary role. These stepfathers tend to parent by observation rather than taking a more hands on approach.

When the Matriarchal couple finds itself showing signs of distress, it is usually when the highly competent wife gets overwhelmed. Sometimes, this is when the couple has a child together. This leads to re-negotiating the division of labor. Since the matriarchal man is often happy with the initial arrangement, this can cause problems and resentments.

Romantic Couple

The third type of stepfamily couple researchers identified is the Romantic Couple.

The Romantic Couple believes they are destined to find each other and to thereby overcome losses suffered from previous marriages. They have more of a fantasy style of relating and are convinced they do not need to talk things out because their deep mutual understanding makes talking unnecessary. This means they probably didn't sort through the tougher issues that arise in every stepfamily—problems with former spouses, parenting-style incompatibilities, even childhood trauma.

Couples in these types of relationships often do not want their former spouses or indeed any non-custodial parents to be involved. Romantics are history revisionists. They often create a family narrative that focuses on the newly merged family and excludes pesky facts about the past they find unsavory or inconvenient.

I have seen all these types of stepfamilies over the years. Dr. Bray's research has helped many couples to understand themselves better.

Unrealistic Expectations

When reality hits and the fog dissipates and suddenly we're not feeling so in love anymore, the next logical step is to assume something is wrong. We tend to look outside ourselves and find fault with our spouse, our biological kids, or our stepkids.

If not identified for what this not-so-in-love feeling is (i.e., the healthy and natural maturation of the relationship), this stage can be challenging to a couple. The urge to blame someone for the death of the fantasy-family dream is nearly irresistible, which is why people blame themselves, their spouses or the children—or get divorced.

> Each family member is sifting and sorting, assessing and re-assessing his or her place in this new family hierarchy.

The problems inherent in the blame game are many, but one of the least understood aspects of blaming other people is that it disempowers the blamer. It's an abdication of responsibility, an abdication of power. If the blamer hands over responsibility for his happiness to some one else, he has automatically deprived himself of the ability to fix it.

This is a precarious time in the development of a new stepfamily. Children—who are naturally less able to process the stress or deal with it maturely—are even more prone to confusion. Each family member is sifting and sorting, assessing and re-assessing his or her place in this new family hierarchy. It is natural to feel off-balance at this point in the process, which is why this next stage is so crucial if the new family is to succeed.

Critical to any family's success is awareness. With this stage comes clarity and acceptance and the realization that, "It's not that something is wrong—it's that we're a stepfamily and we are on a journey."

In fact, my own timetable for hurrying us along contributed significantly to our problems.

This was a huge step for me, personally. Six months into my remarriage, I realized I needed to let go of my fantasy family, my unrealistic expectations for myself, my spouse, and the children. I had to address my fears of not doing things right, just as I had to stop blaming everyone else for my own disappointments. I realized forming this new stepfamily was going to take longer than I thought.

I was stunned when the therapist we were seeing told us the process could take up to five years. I bristled at this and determined to try even harder to beat the odds. We were different and could do it better and faster. In fact, my own timetable for hurrying us along contributed significantly to our problems.

Why Attachment is Key

Because this is primarily a chapter on the importance of the pair-bond, I would like to discuss setting healthy boundaries for the future, especially when you begin to experience the honeymoon fading and you're having to deal with the differences that inevitably come up. Crises and difficulties can erode your bond, and it will take a deliberate effort to repair or rebuild it.

One of the greatest ironies of life is it takes two people to have a workable and healthy relationship and only one person to shake that relationship up.

When a previous relationship implodes, trusting that any relationship can withstand the stresses of life, money, parenting, and exes becomes more difficult. In a way, it defies logic to trust relationships ever again.

This is why learning to recognize how, why, and in what manner attachment occurs within a remarriage is so important.

One of the most emotionally important aspects of how we reach out to others is exemplified in the Still Face Experiment by Dr. Edward Tronick, Ph.D, of Harvard University, which is on YouTube.

The video shows the interaction between a mother and her year-old baby with the baby making the kinds of adorable bids for attention and connection you might expect a baby to make. Each of us experienced bonding on varying levels with our parents or caregivers. Some parents may have done this better than others, but their actions can affect how and with whom we bonded as adults.

If you watch the video, you will see the mother and her baby are very engaged. They have interactions that include looks, smiles, and playful exchanges. Then the mother is asked to face herself away from her baby. When she turns back around to interact with her child, she wears a still, expressionless face.

At first, the baby attempts to get the mother to play again by doing all the adorable things it did before when it got her attention. But the baby is met with only a blank stare. The child squeals and becomes increasingly distressed. As soon as the mother assumes smiling and engaging again, the child calms down.

It's a little agonizing to watch the baby making bids for attention that meet only non-response. But as adults, we make the same bids for attention in subtle, not so subtle, (and sometimes far less adorable) ways.

Is it even possible to be present and engaged with our children and our spouse every waking moment? Can we meet the needs of everyone who calls on us? Of course not. Part of learning how to "do" life is making sure we get our own needs met, too, and accepting that others cannot always be entirely there for us.

Yet research done by the great Dr. John Gottman, Ph.D, shows that newlyweds who stayed married after six years responded positively to bids for attention about eighty-six percent of the time.

Couples that divorced after six years responded to bids only thirty-three percent of the time.

This finding coined the term "emotional bank account," and it's an important concept since what's in a couple's emotional bank account directly affects how they weather storms together as well as the quality of their sexual intimacy.

A bid for attention can be small. It can be as simple as someone saying, "I talked to my brother today"; "Let's cuddle"; "Do I look okay in this dress?"; "Watch a movie with me."; "Let's put the baby down for a nap."

Each of these statements can represent a bid for attention. The subtext could be, "Will you talk to me now?"; "Can I have affection or connection from you?"; "Please tell me I look good."; "Will you spend some time with me?"; or "I really need some help with the baby tonight."

Bids for attention can also include nonverbal gestures like a wink or a smile.

When a stepparent reaches out to a stepchild and is rebuffed with a "still face," or visible annoyance, it is hard not to take that personally. It can be stunning to see the efforts of stepparents reaching out to their stepchildren who are then met with open hostility or the proverbial teenage stonewall.

Alternately, stepparents rebuffing or ignoring bids for attention from their stepchildren can be just as confusing and painful.

Yet biological children may experience their own emotional marooning. A parent may be so excited to be in a new relationship, much of the energy formerly spent on the child is now devoted to the new spouse.

In many situations, a parent and a child may have become codependent. Some parents depend on their children for emotional support during a crisis, a death, or a divorce. Even something as simple as displacing a child who is used to sleeping in the big comfortable "parent bed" and relegating that child back to his old room again can feel like abandonment.

Yet that same kind of abandonment can happen between a husband and wife.

The Insider-Outsider Gap in Stepfamilies

When my husband and I first married, I was excited to have a fresh start. I moved into his house, which had been recently built for him and his child. I relocated one hundred miles away to a new town, new home, and new friends. I'm an adventurous person, so I welcomed the challenge.

However, only a few months into our new marriage, I had an overwhelming sense I'd moved into his life, his work, his friends, and his home. I experienced firsthand what it felt like to hold the "outsider" position in our new stepfamily.

I made the mistake of replacing my child's bedroom curtains and a bedspread which his grandmother had made for him with new furniture and new bedding. It did not take long for me to realize the error of that decision.

My husband and his child were established in this community with their friends. They were insiders. My child and I felt like outsiders.

Insiders can feel uncomfortable, too. They often experience anxiety as they watch their new spouse floundering in new social situations and new environments. Insiders struggle to stay connected to their own children while at the same time remaining connected to their spouses.

In my practice, I have seen stepfamilies which have never been able to recover from the insider-outsider gap, which is a great term coined by researchers. Over the years, many clients have sat down with me and described the pain of never having felt as though they were a part of the stepfamily—of never being able to have a private conversation with a parent after the remarriage; of never having time alone with a parent. Or sometimes the pain of having stepparents who just never accepted them.

Managing the needs of kids, career, and marriage is difficult under the best of circumstances, but at least in a first marriage there is a honeymoon phase without children. In a second marriage, the children are there right from the start. Finding a way to manage all these relationships is a balancing act, especially if you're having to learn how to do it before true bonding has actually occurred.

As we saw with newly marrieds Adele and Peter, moving into the same house after a free-and-easy dating period can be particularly stressful. Decisions have to be made and rules established. Adele may have seemed like more of a friend to her stepchildren at first, but now she was moving into what she thought her role should be, which was as an authority figure. The more overwhelmed she felt, the more she shut down and the greater number of "bids" for attention she ignored.

> However, only a few months into our new marriage, I had an overwhelming sense that I'd moved into his life, his work, his friends, and his home.

Peter did the same. After a stressful week at work, all he could think about was relaxing. Yet in that process, he was pushing away his new wife and occasionally even his kids.

Does that mean we have to martyr ourselves and give up all our interests and hobbies for the sake of the family? Of course not. But an effort must be made every single day to reach out and connect with those who are most important to us, even if those attempts to connect aren't met with open arms. This takes real patience and maturity. But as you now realize after having read this chapter, bids for attention can be greeted with sensitivity and awareness, and it doesn't require a lot of time.

Stepping Stones for the Journey

- Counselors and psychologists who are not familiar with stepfamily dynamics will recommend the couple put themselves first. In first-time marriages, this is true. But in remarriages, this is not true and it can be detrimental to the forming family. Kids must come first. Otherwise, the stress they cause can undermine the developing relationship with your spouse. This is a delicate balancing act. If the only focus is on kids, the marriage bond won't continue.

- The stepfamily couple needs to spend time together alone, and also with children/teens. Researchers agree children are not usually invested in the stepfamily marriage actually working out. Children often hope their original parents will get back together again. Children who have lost a parent to death may fantasize what it would be like if the parent were still alive and both parents were still married.

- Because time is often an issue (as in there is never enough of it, right?), both your new spouse, your children, and stepchildren can end up feeling left out. Arrange alone time with your children, whether they live with you as their primary caregiver or whether you have scheduled visitation. Something as simple as running out to get ice cream together or spending thirty minutes of one-on-one time with your child can help. Try going out to your favorite food truck together, listening to music, hitting golf balls, going for a walk, or playing catch. The child needs to feel like an insider, not an outsider, in your new stepfamily. Discuss this idea with your spouse and brainstorm ideas for your children and his/hers.

- Just as important as spending time alone with your child is spending a few minutes alone with your spouse every day. Turn off technology and resist the urge to discuss high-conflict issues. Do more listening than talking. If things come up, schedule another time to discuss them—this particular togetherness must be a sacred space just the two of you share. If children interrupt, let them know you'll be with them in a few minutes.

- Dating your spouse needs to be a priority. Make sure you and your spouse have a day that is just yours. Resist the temptation to let life encroach upon this time together, no matter how "justifiable" the reason may seem. Dates can be as simple as going to your favorite coffee shop, taking a long walk together, or maybe even going to a fun new restaurant.

- Here's a personal anecdote for you. For many years now, to celebrate our anniversary, my husband and I spend the night downtown and the next day Christmas shopping together. I encourage my client-couples to schedule something special every three months. We all need something to look forward to, and it is all too easy to let the busy-ness of life take over. Any time spent together as a couple should be seen as a necessary investment, like buying car insurance, not a frivolous waste of time and money.

Questions for the Journey

1. Which of the couples in Dr. Bray's research study describe your stepfamily marriage? Neotraditional, Matriarchal or Romantic?

2. How realistic have your expectations been? Have you had to adjust your expectations?

3. Have you experienced being the insider or the outsider? What do you think the children or stepchildren have experienced? Are there ways you can help an outsider become more of an insider?

4. How would you describe your attachment in your family of origin? Whether there was healthy or not so healthy attachment, how has this affected your previous marriage? How has your current marriage been affected?

5. How would you describe your bids for attachment with your spouse? From your spouse to you?

6. Have your considered how your children and/or stepchildren's experience with attachment have affected their relationship with you? With the stepfamily in general?

7. How are you and your spouse doing balancing time for children, in relation to time for the marriage?

———•◦•———

Stepping Stones for Creating Healthy Boundaries

We change our behavior when the pain of staying the same becomes greater than the pain of changing. Consequences give us the pain that motivates us to change.
—Henry Cloud

J ack and Claire were an attractive couple who, previous to settling down and having children, lived in Malibu, California, and worked in the movie industry. They divorced when their son, Matthew, was sixteen years old and their daughter, Scarlett, was fourteen.

There had been serious neglect of the relationship for years, tons of simmering resentment and a readiness (particularly on Jack's part) to jump to conclusions regarding Claire. If he'd been critical of her before their divorce, he was ten times more critical of her now that she'd gotten remarried. Her new husband, Robert, made twice as much money as Jack did, and it irritated him unbearably.

As teens will sometimes do, their children Matthew and Scarlett took full advantage of the situation to get what they wanted—

which in this case were daily trips to Chik-Fil-A or whatever fast food they happened to be craving at the moment. Claire worked long hours, but cared greatly about what her children ate, and naturally this didn't include fast food. The groceries she purchased were always healthy ones. She lovingly prepared snacks for her children to enjoy before she got home.

When they returned from school, Matthew and Scarlett would text their father and tell him they were starving and there was nothing to eat in the house. This incensed Jack, who felt as though all his child support money was being misspent. He decided, erroneously, that Robert was too cheap to feed his kids. Instead of talking to Claire about it, he continued to nurse grievances, just like he did in the old days when they were married.

Grumbling and resentful, he would drive to get food for his hungry teens. Then Claire would come home and fix dinner that no one ate. After a year of this, Claire stopped fixing dinner for her kids and just made dinner for her and Robert. This only served to reinforce Jack's belief that she didn't care about their children and Robert was cheating them, which of course couldn't have been further from the truth.

What was true was that Jack still resented Claire for having left him. He resented her and hated having to pay child support, not only because he couldn't control how the money was spent, but because he figured Robert's salary was more than adequate to cover their expenses, so why should he go broke providing? He saw her relaxed and happy with Robert, and it bothered him. A lot.

He stopped paying his child support, forcing Claire, at great inconvenience, to take him back to court.

It was a long ugly battle between two people who had yet to come to terms with one of the most important facts about marriage, parenthood, and divorce: if you have kids with someone, you are going to be with them for the rest of your life—whether you are married to them or not.

Boundaries are a touchy subject with most people, primarily because people believe their boundaries are inviolable and your boundaries are little more than a suggestion.

That's not exactly the case, is it?

Kids are rarely great respecters of boundaries, and even many adults have a hard time observing them. Yet the establishment of what is and isn't acceptable, especially what information can be shared by children about you to your former spouse is important.

A boundary is defined as a mark or line that determines a stopping or starting place.

Erecting healthy boundaries in a stepfamily can be hindered in a variety of ways.

A child typically visits his non-custodial parent on a court-ordered every-other-weekend schedule. Kids will and do talk. Even in a traditional first marriage, parents can recall embarrassing details their child shared with friends or parents of friends at church, school, or a sporting event. "Look, that lady's butt is even bigger than yours!" a cherub-faced boy once shouted inside a supermarket.

Or my favorite, which came out of the mouth of a little girl I saw at the store one day who had red Pippi Longstocking braids. "Mama, is that lady going to die soon?" she asked about the elderly woman her mom was talking to.

But inappropriate comments are only one form of boundary crossing, and sometimes a mildly funny one at that. Other types might be dropping the kids off earlier than agreed upon, repeatedly missing visitation, purposely withholding child support, or even something like opening a door without knocking.

But it also requires that you balance your emotions with the more rational parts of your brain. And that's a lot tougher than it looks.

Determining where you draw your line is an essential part of feeling respected. It requires staying in touch with how you really feel, which is hard sometimes when you're not used to saying no or believe you don't have the right to say no. But it also requires you balance your emotions with the more rational parts of your brain. And that's a lot tougher than it looks.

A lovely client of mine, Gail, now a stepmother herself, recalled her early manipulative efforts to play one parent against the other. As a young teen, she frequently threatened to go live with her biological father. One day, her stepfather called her bluff. He created a definite boundary and dared her to cross it by picking up the phone to call her father and then ordering her to pack her bags.

Make no mistake—her bluff was called. She did not want to change residences and begged him to put down the phone. He told her to stop her nonsense and to never again say she wanted to move out. Humbly, she agreed. While this worked for this stepfather, in other stepfamilies this could be a disaster. Each stepfamily is different. What works for one, may not work for another.

Today, that same stepfamily is thriving. Its members do not define themselves as a stepfamily. Time, relationship building, and memory building laid down a wonderful foundation of love and caring that has sustained them over many years.

Boundaries are about fixing, changing and controlling you, not others. You will never be able to control other people. Influence them, perhaps. Even guide them to a certain degree. But eventually, the controllees often rebel against the controllers. If there's any confusion on this subject, think back to your own adolescence!

Coming to terms with our inability to change people is the better part of wisdom.

One of the biggest favors you can do yourself and others is to sit down, write out all the things you wish were different about your spouse or your kids and then take a long hard look at the ways you've been trying to change them.

You may never change them, but you can influence and role model healthy boundaries.

However, when other people have been informed of what your boundaries are and persist in crossing them, you have to consider your next step.

Realize, of course, that you become a nag if you keep insisting. At some point, you must figure out how you will respect your own boundaries if others won't. For instance, if the kids won't respect your boundary about them cleaning their dropped food wrappers out of the car—and you've asked them kindly several times—you might think about respecting your own boundary by refusing to let them eat food in the car.

But it is also good to be vigilant for signs you are violating other people's boundaries. Can you hear and respect when your spouse sets a boundary with you? When you have teenage children, what's a "violation of boundaries" and what's "good parenting" becomes an ever-fluctuating line.

Consider the example of a stepfamily of six I counseled—Laura and Zach. Two of the teens were Zach's and two of the preteens were Laura's.

The couple recently discovered that Zach's fifteen-year-old daughter had been skipping school, failing several classes, and hanging out with a crowd that Laura, in particular, didn't like. She suffered anguish over this since she'd begun acting out herself at around her stepdaughter's age. Her parents did not confront her or set limits to help get her back on the right track, so she felt doubly compelled to help Zach redirect his wayward daughter.

Laura had paid dearly for her high school distractions and poor decision making. Her shabby grades kept her from getting into a decent college and she had been forced to slave away at a series of minimum-wage jobs before finally going to night school. Laura was also rightfully concerned about how her stepdaughter's behavior might affect her younger stepsiblings.

The issue of what to do about the girl's behavior put Laura and Zach at odds with one another. Zach had a laidback parenting style. He'd experimented with drinking and smoking when he was a kid and felt that as a successful businessman now, he'd grown up just fine, regardless of whatever "fool things" he'd done. According to him, Laura's concerns were overblown.

Laura did her best to encourage Zach to set some guidelines for his daughter, but he refused. She resented Zach for ignoring her recommendations and for dismissing her concerns. Six months later, the family was still in turmoil.

Laura eventually realized that Zach was never going to see it her way. She could set as many boundaries as she liked, but since her stepdaughter was ultimately Zach's responsibility, she had no real authority over how to parent the girl. Controlling Zach or the girl was out of the question.

The only person she could control was herself.

So she created an emotional boundary when her stepdaughter came home with another disappointing report card. She chose not to allow the situation to affect her personally, like it once did. Creating this boundary allowed her to deal with her own emotional baggage from her past. When she felt herself getting worked up about it, she took a deep breath and remembered that responsibility for the stepdaughter was not hers. It was Zach's and the girl's mother.

> **Creating this boundary allowed her to deal with her own emotional baggage from her past.**

This emotional boundary also allowed her to clarify to her own children what her expectations were for them. "Letting go, in a way, allowed me to disconnect from the problem and reconnect with my husband," Laura said.

So how do you rediscover your peace-of-mind once something hurtful or anger-causing has set up an outpost inside your head?

1. Accept once and for all that other people do not see the world the same way that you do.

2. When you're thwarted in your ability to get people to see things your way, try to look for support from someone who has been there, someone who can help you gain perspective on the situation. Not your perspective, of course; the other person's perspective. Sometimes having someone else explain it to you helps. You're less defensive and more likely to listen.

3. Seek help from a trusted professional. Sometimes the only way to let go or process an issue is to talk it out with a therapist or your local pastor.

Children who share personal information about you to the other parent or the extended family make you feel as though you have no control over anything going on inside your house. This can be embarrassing at best, infuriating at worst, but it can expose you to a fair amount of criticism, whether that criticism is warranted or merely the byproduct of a faulty interpretation of the facts.

It is wise to remember some children share out of a sense of loyalty to the other parent. And some parents (maybe with good reason and maybe not) actively snoop, either from resentful curiosity or for the child's own protection.

Some of that sharing is, no doubt, innocent. But when kids get older, they may be looking for validation. Manipulation can be a part of some children or teens' agendas.

Make no mistake—these things happen in original families, too. Eventually, most parents realize what the child is doing and take steps to correct it.

But stepfamilies are at a disadvantage. Unless former spouses are cordial and know how to effectively co-parent, discord, manipulation, and unhealthy sharing of information can create significant problems (as we saw with Claire and Jack).

You can get ahead of this if you are practicing healthy boundaries. You're never going to not have problems. Life never adheres to the hard-and-fast rules of football—there are no time outs (not for you, anyway), no consistently thrown penalty flags, and no end zone where you can spike the ball. Things can get better. In fact, in many stepfamilies, once the kids leave home, life often becomes easier for the couple. But understanding your boundaries will help you along every stepping stone of your journey, both within your family and within the larger world.

If parenting is tough, then stepparenting is Hall of Fame material.

For many people, just knowing that makes them feel better. Many of us wander around thinking we're the only ones who are getting it wrong. Nothing could be further from the truth. We're all out here doing the best we can, even if our best is sometimes woefully inadequate. When we know better, we do better.

Until then, all we can do is proceed with compassion.

> Life never adheres to the hard-and-fast rules of football—there are no time outs (not for you, anyway), no consistently thrown penalty flags, and no end zone where you can spike the ball.

> But understanding your boundaries will help you along every stepping stone of your journey, both within your family and within the larger world.

Questions for the Journey

1. What did you learn about boundaries growing up in your home? Were there walls, fences, or no boundaries at all?

2. What do boundaries look like in your personal life? What do they look like in your stepfamily life?

3. Are you aware when you violate or disrespect another person's boundaries?

4. What have been the most difficult boundary issues in your stepfamily?

5. Have you experienced rigidity or flexibility in determining what boundaries are realistic in your stepfamily?

6. When your boundaries are not respected, what kinds of emotional, physical or spiritual adjustments do you make? Do you have a trusted friend, mentor, pastor, support group, or professional counselor to whom you can go when you need objective feedback about an issue?

———•·•———

CHAPTER 5

Stepping Stones for Healthy Parenting
in a Stepfamily

When we are no longer able to change a situation, we are
challenged to change ourselves.

—**Victor Frankl**

When it comes to attachment in stepfamilies, the concept of TIME cannot be underestimated. It takes time for a stepfamily to bond. There is no particular timeframe for this because each family is unique. But most experts agree it takes at least five to seven years.

I have created an acronym to help readers remember the key aspects of attachment in stepfamilies:

T	Tolerance for the new paths each person is taking in the new family.
I	Insight into your own thoughts, feelings and experiences within the stepfamily.
M	Meaningful Activity and Memory Making, with an eye toward sorting out what works for each family member.
E	Empathy, which requires you to consider what it's like for each child (and your new spouse) to build emotional bridges during a difficult transition.

The good news is this: in some cases, the bond between a stepparent and a stepchild can run very deep.

Sometimes a stepparent makes a greater investment of time, emotion and energy than the biological parent does, even though that investment can feel like a job no one notices or appreciates.

It can be work without immediate reward.

But a lot of this is predicated on which home the child primarily resides in. For instance, some kids are only at the house on the weekends and even then, they may spend the majority of their time with their biological parent.

In terms of stepfamily dynamics, there is a huge difference between visiting kids and kids who live full-time with one parent.

Such a stepparent was my client, Mark. A loving and conscientious man, he found himself struggling to define his role in his stepchild's life. This struggle was made harder by the fact that he had been a stepson himself once upon a time.

"I don't like the word 'stepmom' or 'stepdad,'" Mark explains. "I think words like that just create a barrier. I liked to think of my mom as 'mom.' That's what she always was to me. My biological mother died when I was a toddler. Technically, she may have been a stepparent, but she did a great deal for me.

"But looking back, I realize that she walled herself off emotionally. She took care of all my childhood needs, but she kept me at a distance. She did this, I believe, because she was afraid that

I would reject her at some point, or that I wouldn't love her in return.

"For most of my life, I blamed her for the lack of real connection in our relationship, but after I became a stepparent myself, I gained a greater understanding of the dynamics that occur when you try to merge two families into one. Maybe this trial was a necessary one for me. Otherwise, I would have never understood what my stepmother had been going through. I would have lived with a kind of low-grade resentment for the rest of my life.

"When Joanna and I married, we each had a child from our previous marriages. We knew nothing we did could replace the other parent, and there were built-in limitations to our roles.

"What worked for us was being flexible. I came up with the term, 'Rubber-Band Dad.' In other words, I had to learn to be comfortable investing my time and my heart into a child who still had primary loyalties to his biological father.

"The only problem is, this is so much easier to preach than it is to practice.

"I had a somewhat unique perspective because I was both an adult stepchild and I was also in the process of ushering a stepchild into adulthood. I believe that the biggest hindrance to good relationships in stepfamilies is the fear of being hurt. If you let yourself become emotionally attached, you become emotionally vulnerable. It's that simple.

"Even though I knew going in that our situation was bound to be a challenging one, what I hadn't anticipated was that I would end up caring so deeply.

"The moment that really brought me to my knees came after I'd spent long hours helping my stepson with a project. When he received recognition for his work, without even thinking about it, he turned to his dad to celebrate with him.

"That hurt me profoundly. It angered me. I'm not proud of my reaction—celebrating with his biological father was absolutely the right and natural thing for any boy to do—but that experience helped me understand what my own stepmother must have feared. "I loved my stepson. But I wondered and agonized, did he love me back?

"It is painful to put your whole heart into a relationship and then have to step back because you aren't the 'real mom' or the 'real dad.'"

"If fear makes it hard for adults to love someone, think how risky it must be for their children.

> It is painful to put your whole heart into a relationship and then have to step back because you aren't the "real mom" or the "real dad".

"Two things, I think, kept me from reaching out to my mom. First, after my own mother died, I was afraid of losing another mother. Second, I felt guilty about loving someone else. It felt as though I were betraying my mother's memory.

"I think so much misunderstanding could have been avoided if someone had just reassured me that it was okay, really okay, to love my stepmom."

> I think so much misunderstanding could have been avoided is someone had just reassured me that it was okay, really okay, to love my stepmom.

Love is always a risk, but as a therapist—as a human being—I believe loving is what we are put on this planet to do. We must learn to love without hope of reward. We must learn to love not because someone is "deserving," but because they are human. Just like we are.

Children can be generous. An adult who proceeds patiently with them and without resorting to anger, blame, or name-calling automatically lays the initial groundwork for love, which is called respect.

Remember where you were when you were that age. Do the words "confused" and "angry" ring a bell? Teens, especially, may look like adults, but they are not adults. Most of them (emotionally at least) are little more than toddlers masquerading as grownups.

If we can learn to become less reactive to what's being thrown at us, behavior-wise, we will find it easier to proceed in a rational manner. That starts with taking care of ourselves—enough sleep, healthier eating, more exercise, journaling, and avoiding mood-altering substances like drugs and alcohol.

Behave like an adult, lead by example, and you will eventually receive what you have coming to you, even if that seems like a long time from now. The key element for stepfamilies to remember is this whole process takes time.

> **The key element for stepfamilies to remember is that this whole process takes time.**

To Be Respected, You Must Be Worthy of that Respect

Children are insightful and observant. They see what's going on, even if they can't always articulate it properly or let you know they appreciate the effort being made on their behalf.

Love joins both action and emotion.

Feelings cannot be manufactured. They must develop over time.

How we choose to act, however, is within our immediate control.

Define your role as a stepparent with your spouse. Talk through how you both want this to look. Be willing to be flexible re-evaluate, and re-adjust your role. Spend time listening. Keep a sense of humor. And perhaps, most importantly, be patient. If you stick with it, you will see long term rewards you could not have ever imagined.

Part of the problem inherent in all stepfamilies is the spouses don't have an equal relationship with their stepchildren. This creates an imbalance in the family dynamic that can make things pretty stressful for all involved, including first spouses.

As children and teens are adjusting to a stepparent, they must also learn to respect this new adult in their lives. Respect can be an uphill climb. There is a delicate balance between allowing children to express their emotions or attitudes about their stepparent and showing them basic respect.

For instance, if a stepparent has to take the children to the store while the biological parent is at work and the child insists on running out into the street, the stepparent must intervene. It's an obvious safety issue.

Other situations may not be so clear. If a child is surly, there are times to ignore such behavior and there are times when it must be addressed. Before discussing it with your spouse, take time to journal and process. Try to present with the reporter technique mentioned in the chapter on Stepping Stones for Resolving Conflict.

How to Tell Your Kids Some Sticky Truths

> We must remember that if we say things that are damaging or negative about the other parent, we are obliquely criticizing that child,

If we were wronged in our first marriage, the temptation to tell our kids the truth about what happened (i.e., the spouse had an affair, there was substance abuse, etc.) can be overwhelming. The problem is our kids, especially teens, will often take on that shame and internalize it. It is to the child's detriment to hear what a parent did because a child will say to himself, "My parent is flawed. Therefore, I must be flawed, too."

We must remember if we say things which are damaging or negative about the other parent, we are obliquely criticizing that child.

Yet telling children the truth—as potentially damaging or hurtful as that truth may be—may be beneficial if it validates a child's past or current knowledge.

For instance, if a parent had a chemical addiction or some type of behavior which was equally destructive, and your child asks questions about it, you need to be honest and validate that reality. To deny something our children have witnessed or experienced can instill in them an inability to trust their own experience of reality. It's called gas-lighting.

As parents, it is vital we only share as much age-appropriate information as a child needs to hear.

Case in point: my client Tracey, whose ex-husband had recently been arrested for having sex with a sixteen-year-old girl.

Tracey came in to see me during a particularly stressful period in her life, looking for guidance on how best to handle this specific situation. She was a single mom who had full custody of her twelve-year-old son and eight-year-old daughter. They both loved their father, Phillip, but the circumstances of their visitation with him had dramatically changed.

According to the laws of Texas, Phillip was to be given "supervised visitation" only. That meant only under Tracey's roof and with only Tracey or another approved caretaker in the room. If Tracey had to go to the restroom, Phillip was legally obligated to step outside the house until she was done. He could no longer take his kids to McDonald's or indeed any restaurant or drive-thru where there might be a Play Place or any area dedicated to children. He had to change residences because he lived too close to the neighborhood pool.

Tracey had no idea how to tell her children what had happened or why it was they could no longer go over to Daddy's on the weekend. She was boiling with resentment over his compulsive sexual behavior and the damage he had done not just to his own children but the young girl he had taken advantage of.

By working together, we found a way to slowly introduce the truth to Tracey's children using age-appropriate guidelines. Tracey learned how to answer her kids' questions with facts and few embellishments. But if they asked, she made it her business to answer.

What she told them was Daddy had broken the law and was now being supervised by special law enforcement agents. He had to live a very restricted life and wouldn't be allowed to see his kids unsupervised, for a number of years.

She was careful to say Phillip loved them and nothing he'd done had anything to do with them. But she also emphasized if they ever felt uncomfortable with Phillip or if he touched them or talked to them in a way that felt uncomfortable, no matter what he told them might happen if they said anything to her or another adult, they needed to tell her at once. She repeated this last part many times.

Tracey knew that as her kids got older, their questions were going to get a lot more specific. She practiced in advance how she would answer these questions.

By observing his probation, taking frequent polygraph tests and going to his court-ordered therapy, Phillip demonstrated how eager he was to prove himself trustworthy to society at large, and his family in particular. He also joined Alcoholics Anonymous so his judgment would no longer be impaired by excessive drinking.

These types of family situations are fraught with peril. A potential landmine seems to hide around every corner. But with help and time and patience, even something this awful can be worked through.

> It is vital that we, as parents, proceed carefully and choose a way to share information and details without causing more pain.

Yet to deny something our children have witnessed or experienced can create within them a sense of confusion. It fosters an inability for children to trust their own perceptions.

It is vital that we, as parents, proceed carefully and choose a way to share information and details without causing more pain. Continuing to remind our children or teens about the other parent's shortfalls or choices is never productive.

Again, how, when, and why we share information is so important. Even abused children sometimes try to protect an abusive parent. It hurts not to be loved the way all children want to be loved.

In matters where a child may be in danger, consider how to give your child enough information to keep him or her safe. Some children or teens may have an incredibly difficult time hearing such hard truths.

If a situation presents an immediate threat to your child, you must call 911 or local sheriff's department. In certain situations, you may need to consult an attorney. This is for your protection as well as theirs. If the law finds you complicit in someone else's illegal behavior, your silence can be as damning as their guilt.

Sexual Abuse within the Stepfamily

Sexual abuse can happen in any family. Research studies show varying results of the occurrence of sexual abuse in first time families versus stepfamilies. Regardless, it is sobering when sexual abuse occurs. Researchers report different statistics for biological parents who abuse and stepparents who abuse. Some show a higher rate for stepparents than biological parents and others report higher rates of abuse by biological parents. There are many factors in the research world and how they come to such different conclusions. Complicating matters is how sexual abuse is defined and the fact that sexual abuse is not always reported.

Unfortunately, my client, Colin, was a victim of sexual abuse by his stepfather.

Colin was ten years old when his mother remarried. For a while, everything seemed to be okay. He was happy that his mother had found a partner, and James, his new stepdad, was an easy-going guy. Sometimes James would take Colin bowling or fishing. Once they got tickets to a football game. Colin was grateful for the attention. His own father lived out-of-state and Colin rarely heard from him.

Twice a week, Colin's mother, a nurse, worked the night shift. That left Colin and James alone together. When James started walking around without any clothes on, Colin felt uncomfortable, but he thought maybe it was just locker room behavior and that he was stressing out about it for no reason.

The sexual abuse began when James walked into Colin's bedroom one night. He warned Colin that telling his mother would put her in terrible danger because James would kill her and Colin, too, if he had to.

Colin believed him. He was petrified.

As Colin got older, the abuse continued. He was getting into a lot of fights at school and at home, acting out because he felt angry, abandoned, and ashamed. Alcohol and drugs became fixtures in his young life—anything not to have to think about what was happening to him at home. Colin started staying out at night, sleeping in parked cars or on friends' couches. His mother was crazy with worry but still had no idea what was going on.

Then, on one of the few days Colin went to school, a social worker came to his Health Science class and spoke about sexual abuse within families. Colin's head pounded. He thought he was going to black out. After class was over, he couldn't stand up from his desk. His teacher asked him what was wrong—and that's when it all came rushing out.

The school called his mother and she came at once. Devastated to learn what had been happening right in her own home, she and the school counselor called CPS together. Colin was fortunate she believed him. There are times when a parent's first reaction to news of sexual abuse is to deny it or to insist the child is lying.

Child Protective Services helped make arrangements for Colin and his mother to go somewhere else while the stepfather was dealt with legally. This is important. No child should stay in the same house with his or her abuser.

The best safeguard you have as a parent trying to protect your child is to talk to them about the potential for abuse. Don't scare them. Just keep telling them if an adult tries to touch them or talks to them in a way that feels icky, no matter what that adult says might happen, the child will always be safe discussing these things with you.

Give the child a safe space. And be vigilant.

Sexual Issues that May Present in the Stepfamily

Sexual issues can occur in any family—rich or poor, college educated or high school dropout. It is best if the couple is aware of how their displays of affection and manner of dress impact the children at home.

Being circumspect about your private life is an important boundary. It can be odd for children of any age to see their parents with another person, much less in a passionate, intimate manner.

Young children are curious and they are capable of engaging in inappropriate sexual behavior. This can happen between biological siblings, but can also happen between step-siblings. That's one of the reasons why it is important to monitor children and teens of all ages. Boundaries concerning appropriate clothing and respecting closed doors are only a few of the important issues in any home. Should something happen in your home between children, it is important to address it. Don't avoid it. Get professional help to determine the next steps.

Danger Situations for Children and Teens

If a child reports a parent is driving under the influence while that child is in the custody of the parent, action needs to be taken immediately.

You will need to proceed with caution because the situation is potentially volatile. People are hardly their rational best when they've been drinking or taking drugs.

But the good news is a child can be tracked on his cellphone. Technology exists which will enable you to find that child's exact location. Experts recommend you "accidentally" show up at the place where your child has been taken and then calmly—and I can't stress this enough—calmly remove your child from this dangerous situation. But if there is a potentially life-threatening situation, you must call 911 for immediate assistance. Don't try to handle it on your own.

An adult is required to report suspected neglect or child abuse to the proper authorities, such as Child Protective Services. Each state has an agency which investigates these reports, and in some states, reports can be filed anonymously. Consulting with a reputable family law attorney can give you information on the laws in your state and when and if you need to address issues from a legal perspective.

Stepping Stones for the Journey

- Stepfamilies with only one parent having children can be easier to deal with than each spouse having children. Experts call this a simple versus complex stepfamily. Bringing two family cultures, two parenting styles, children with different needs, talents, and personalities takes intentional effort and time to merge.

- Biological parents and their respective family culture can complicate any stepfamily dynamic. If your former spouse marries, now their spouse, their children, and all the above-mentioned dynamics increase again.

- Determining how to parent and create stepfamily rules is critical. Adults need to take into consideration whether the children are full time, part-time or if there is joint custody. Experts agree if children visit part-time or even only on holidays—and they live far enough away, they don't need the same rules as the children who are there on a regular basis.

- Be aware that different sets of rules can be confusing for children traveling between homes. The rules at one house can be lax at one parent's house and strict at another's. Do your best to not criticize how the other parents run their home.

- Non-residential parents often sometimes struggle because they have less time with their own children. Some have difficulty connecting with their full-time stepchildren out of subconscious or conscious loyalty to their own children.

- Parents who have custody of their children can also have loyalty conflicts with stepchildren who are residential or non-residential. It can be very difficult to manage all the needs and differences between children in the home.

- Mothers and fathers have been known to be protective of their children and even consciously or subconsciously block a stepparent from connecting. Parents can put limitations on the relationship with a stepparent for a variety of reasons. The bond between a parent and child runs deep and it takes place before the stepfamily marriage.

- It is a mistake to assume that as the stepparent, you have authority just because you are an adult. Leave the disciplining to your stepchild's biological parents. If they refuse to discipline, discuss it with them, but don't let yourself hold out much hope that things will change right away or at all. It is best to adjust your own perceptions and attitudes and to extricate yourself emotionally from the situation. Control what you can, which is you. If you want more out of your relationship with your stepchildren, be willing to invest more of your time, patience, and effort.

- Use your best communication skills to discuss parenting issues with your current spouse and his/her former spouse— use caution when asking for advice from him/her during whatever discussions you may be having with your spouse. Only do this if your spouse is asking for extra support. No matter how tactfully handled, someone may feel ganged up on. If there are things you need to say, say them with diplomacy but never in front of the kids and never in front of your stepchildren's other biological parent.

Janet Nicholas

- When possible, go the extra mile to befriend your spouse's ex, which can give you more leverage with the kids. You can let the parent know that you support them and their role as a caregiver. But of course, in some situations this won't be possible on any level.

- If you get in between your spouse and his biological child during an argument, however justified, you may be inviting that child to resent you. It's a slippery slope. Obviously, if the argument escalates into violence, that's an entirely separate issue, but for any run-of-the-mill arguments, it pays to stay out of them. Keep your focus on the stepping stone that is least likely to knock you off your path. Best intentions can, and often do, backfire. Maybe all you do is go tsk tsk when your husband argues with his fourteen-year-old daughter over her sudden interest in boys and makeup. Maybe the daughter makes an open appeal to you for aid. A good answer could be: "I'm going to let you two handle it." It's important they find a way of navigating these waters together. Intervening will rob them of the means to solve problems in the future. Discuss these things in private with your spouse, but don't do it in front of anyone else.

———•◦•———

Questions for the Journey

1. What thoughts and feelings came up for you as you read this chapter?

2. Have you ever struggled with loyalty conflicts over your child/children and your stepchildren?

3. How have you and your spouse navigated your step-family rules in your house? Are you open and flexible about changing the rules when needed?

4. Have you experienced any challenges with your ex or your spouse's ex on parenting differences? If so, what impact has it had on the children, on your marriage?

5. What has been your experience with residential versus non-residential children in your stepfamily?

6. What one area mentioned in this chapter would you like to work on?

7. What one area mentioned in this chapter did you feel as though you were doing well on?

———•◆•———

Stepping Stones for Resolving Conflict

*If you can find a path with no obstacles, it probably doesn't
lead to anywhere.*

〜

—**Unknown**

One of the most pain-filled sessions I ever sat through as a
therapist was with a family from Baton Rouge, Louisiana.
The mother, Yvonne, had lost her previous husband to a
rare form of cancer. Her son, Evan, a popular and athletic boy, was
twelve. Her daughter, Celeste, was an introverted girl of nine.

The father had been greatly beloved by multitudes of friends
and family, and his passing created crippling hardship, both emotionally and financially, for the family he left behind.

But when a door closes, a window often opens, and Yvonne's
sheer emotional rawness made her receptive to love and support where
she found it, which in this case was several years later with a teacher at
Evan's school. Todd was kind, patient, and a dead ringer for her late husband, whose name (Tom) was eerily similar as well. Both men were about
six feet, brown haired, blue-eyed, with an unusual cleft in their chins.

Yvonne claimed not to have noticed the strong resemblance to her late husband, but her children did. Neither Evan nor Celeste could look him in the eyes. Every time they saw Todd, it felt like they were losing their father all over again, losing him and then having to make do with what they considered to be a shabby substitute.

To make matters worse, Todd's wife had remarried a man of considerable means. Todd's daughter, Melanie, who came over on weekends, suffered none of the deprivations that Yvonne's kids had gone through. Melanie was seen as an outsider, and every good thing that happened to her was jealously noted by Celeste and, to a lesser degree, Evan.

Yvonne and Todd struggled to make ends meet, and Todd admitted that in a foolish attempt to keep up with his daughter's new lifestyle, he went a little overboard when his daughter came to visit. This also placed undue strain on the new family.

But this was nothing compared to the pain I saw on the faces of Yvonne, Evan, and Celeste during the first few months I counseled them.

Yvonne's kids just couldn't get past the idea that life had cheated them. One day, they'd had an intact family. They'd had a father who made a good living, took them on fun adventures and loved them unreservedly. The next day, their father was dead and their mother was a ghost of her former self. They were forced to move from a spacious house in the suburbs into a tiny apartment. Then a "replacement dad" came along who even had the nerve to look like their deceased father.

The problem was, as a family, they'd never mourned. Yvonne thought it was wrong to let her children see her cry. She wrongly believed you had to "keep it together" in front of your kids or they might see how frail you were inside, how scared and uncertain and broken.

Yet it is the reverse that's true. Children learn what appropriate emotional responses are from watching their parents. While it's always good to say, "I'm really sad right now, but I want you to know

I'm not going to fall apart and everything is going to be okay," you are also permitted to be emotional in front of your family.

So we grieved. For six months, they came in to see me, and we grieved. Some people are so frozen with sorrow, it takes them a while to thaw.

Yvonne and her children kept journals. Slowly, they began to give themselves permission to feel all the loss and anger that was buried during their brave attempts at coping. And because Todd, their new stepfather, was a patient, empathetic man, he never put any pressure on them to change. Everyone was allowed to heal at his own rate of recovery. Todd had made a commitment to see this thing through.

His patience was ultimately rewarded.

Todd knew there'd been a breakthrough when Evan, without bothering to define the exact nature of his relationship with Todd, referred to him as "my dad" while talking to his coach on the football field.

One day while Todd was napping on the sofa, Celeste and Melanie took some nail polish and painted each of his toenails a different color. Instead of being annoyed by it, Todd recognized it for what it was—a playful step forward. An opportunity for the girls to bond over shared mischief. Progress.

> Todd had made a commitment to see this thing through. His patience was ultimately rewarded.

It took time to get to this point. And time is one thing I don't see a lot of my clients making allowances for. Many people think that a few cathartic episodes spent in my office and everything should be hunky-dory again. It rarely works that way.

For some people who lose a loved one, especially a spouse or a child, the pain is so intolerable, the best they can hope to do is find a way to disconnect and move on.

When Parents Are Excluded from a Child's Life

There are plenty of parents who are shut out of their children's lives not because of death, but because of varying states of animosity between exes. Sometimes the psychological warfare one parent exerts on the children is extremely subtle—a comment here, a comment there. Remarks dropped into conversations with other adults that the kids overhear.

Some parents try to maintain a relationship with their children regardless of how excluded they feel. I encourage such parents to stay involved in whatever ways are available to them.

Arrange for parent-teacher meetings and always know how your child is doing in school. Even if you live out of state, in today's world there are numerous ways to connect with teachers and with your children. Visit as often as you can.

Children need to know you love and value them.

If you are in a situation where you are being blocked from seeing your children, be consistent in your attempts to stay in contact. Even if packages and mail are returned, make sure you keep these packages and date them. One day, your children will be grown and curious. Chances are, they will want to know if you cared enough to try to reconnect with them.

Be respectful if they choose not to reciprocate. Take it slow. But if you are to ever have a relationship with them, it will likely be on their terms, not your own.

Trouble with Your Ex

One of the biggest favors you can do for yourself, your ex, and your kids is to minimize potential opportunities for conflict.

What that means is when there's trouble with your ex, be

smart about it. Limit your means of communication. Face-to-face meetings often have the most potential for conflict. Avoid them.

But when you must meet in person, do so in a neutral environment like a restaurant. People often behave better when they are in public. You have the ability to leave safely if things don't go well.

I don't suggest sending your ex any long emails. In this case, the forced brevity of a text is actually a blessing. Stick to the facts. Don't rehash history. Don't veer off topic.

But as a rule, I don't recommend putting too much in writing. If your ex has a poor memory or if they are manipulative, a brief text or email is a safe option. But sometimes a phone call (with proper voice inflection and intonation) can work and leaves less opportunity for misinterpretation. A call allows for the necessary back and forth that text or email does not allow. I have worked with stepfamilies where the current spouse is able to work with their stepchildren's parent. For a variety of reasons, some divorced couples cannot get out of their old, unhealthy communication patterns. When positive communication happens, it is good for all.

When emotions are running high between exes, I do sometimes encourage my clients to write that person a letter, but don't mail it. Instead, describe any negative thoughts or feelings you are having toward the other person in a journal entry. Try to include everything you've ever wanted to say but didn't or couldn't. Be honest about what you're feeling.

Next, destroy the pages. Let this signify you are releasing your high emotions about the situation or person.

The day after (if what you need to say won't fit into a text) when you've had time to cool down, sit down again and write a brief, factual communication to your ex about the problem at hand. Read it through and have a trusted friend or mentor read through it. You will find you are in a far better head space and less prone to lash out. That alone must be considered a victory.

Writing anything while you're angry, whether to an ex or the phone company or even a politically loaded Facebook rant, is never smart, is it? How many times have we done this only to wake up the next morning, slap one hand over our eyes and groan, "Oh, no. What on earth have I done?"

You must work at forgiving. We all have to work at forgiving. The problem is, half the time, we're not even aware of how sad, angry, or still how hurt we are. This is not bad or wrong, it just is. So give yourself permission to keep working through it—no shaming yourself, please.

Remember that regardless of what your ex-spouse does, you can take responsibility for yourself and refuse to succumb to a power struggle. Sometimes that power struggle is an old familiar waltz of dysfunction a former spouse keeps trying to dance to.

Forgiveness doesn't necessarily mean you trust again, although in certain cases when people teach us new and positive things about them, trust can evolve. While forgiveness may be an active wish on our part and we may take steps to free ourselves from anger, sadness or hurt, remember forgiveness is for the forgiver. Forgiveness is a process that grows over time.

It's not enough to just announce one day to our friends and family that we've "forgiven and moved on." Few things are more poisonous than trying to skip over the grief process and just get straight to forgiveness part without taking at least some of the steps to get there.

How to Deal with Really Unreasonable Exes

If demands are made and you end up having to defend yourself against unreasonable claims and accusations, consider the possibility that things may go from bad to worse. Threats of taking the children away are coin of the realm in such situations, and I know how panic-inducing those threats can be.

I had a client who was so worried that her ex-husband would make good on his promise to take her son away, she used to leave church early and then rush back to the nursery every Sunday just to make sure he was still there. The anxiety she experienced caused her many sleepless, tear-soaked nights.

Don't respond right away. Let things calm down before you do.

Try to be the actor, not the reactor.

No response from you may escalate things at first, but after a while, even the angriest ex has no choice but to calm down.

If there's no one to yell at, you eventually stop yelling.

If you are one of many parents who shares custody with an angry, unreasonable ex, expect that ex to tell anyone who will listen a host of negative things about you. You will want to defend yourself when lies are vigorously and maliciously spread, but it is one of the true injustices of life that defending yourself against liars won't put a stop to the lies.

Lashing out at anybody never makes you look rational.

But take heart. Healthy people who have owned their issues don't say mean things about other people.

Unhappy people are hurting inside. So, when your ex goes for the gusto, it is more an indication of how much pain they are in (not necessarily from you) and may be less of an indication of what's going on between you two at the time. Often, they have unresolved grief or leftovers of their own they're dealing with. Understanding this will enable you to rise above their poor behavior and regain a sense of balance in the relationship.

Stumbling Stones — Danger Words

Just as we have stepping stones along our journey, we also have stumbling stones.

Oddly, we humans learn more from our mistakes than we do from our successes, so try not to see these stumbling stones as a negative.

They aren't. They're a gift.

I spend a lot of time teaching clients what I refer to as "danger words." There are about seven of those, in no particular order. These can be helpful in your relationships with your spouse, your children, stepchildren and other family. They can also help in your work life.

- Why
- You
- Always
- Never
- Should
- Would
- Could

Observe how often you use these words and in what context. This will take some real dedication on your part because you will find each one of these words cropping up in your everyday conversation. So what makes them particularly dangerous?

———— • ————

Stumbling Stone — *WHY*

Any time you ask a person why, you are putting that person in the position of having to defend himself. It's an intimidating word, a word that demands immediate justification for any thought, action, or behavior. "Why did you do that?"

Are there any good answers to that question?

If you're on the receiving end of why, how often do you find yourself panicking a little and stumbling over your answer? Why can also feel as if you are being parented by the other person. Your kneejerk reaction may be to deny or justify.

———— • ————

Stepping Stone — Replacements for *WHY*

Here are some replacements for why:

- When
- Where
- What
- How
- Please tell me more …

Let's say your spouse says something hurtful. Instead of yelling or defending, see what happens when you use the following statements or questions.

"Tell me what was going on with you last night."

"I felt hurt and misunderstood when I tried talking to you about the kids."

"What was your take on what they said?"

"Where do you see us heading on this issue?"

Remember, your goal is to invite your spouse into the conversation, not to shut them down.

———————

Stumbling Stone — *YOU*

The word you creates an automatic retaining wall. There is so much stuff we pile on top of you.

- "You never listen to me."
- "You always say that."
- "If you had done what I asked you to, we wouldn't be in this mess."

So what do I recommend replacing you with? *I.*

- "I'm worried that ..."
- "I felt hurt by ..."
- "I get really insecure when ..."

I is the antidote to you.

During regular communication, of course, you can't avoid using the word you. But you can be more conscious of how you use it. And if you are prone to using it at the beginning of a sentence, nine times out of ten you are headed for trouble and communication will likely be hampered.

Stumbling Stone — Should, Would and Could

Don't these words sound as though they're straight out of a parenting playbook?

- "I told you we should have left thirty minutes ago."
- "You should wear less makeup."
- "If you did your homework, you wouldn't get those kinds of grades."
- "We could have nice things if you weren't so clumsy."

Any time you use the words should, would, or could in a scolding manner, especially to another adult, you are giving yourself an air of superiority. What's implied is that you know better than they do.

Stumbling Stone — Always and Never

The problem with always and never is they are seldom correct.

- "You always do that."
- "You are never there for me."
- "You always take her side."
- "You never take me anywhere."

Now see what happens when you use the words always and never in a positive way.

- "You are always there for me."
- "Thank you for never giving up on us."
- "You always have the best ideas."
- "I have never met anyone like you."

This new script will feel unnatural at first. You may even resent the suggestion of using "better" words. What's wrong with the words you usually say? But as you hone your skill with rapport-building language, it will become very apparent that watching how you express yourself will save you a lot of frustration later on. It may even be exciting to see how people begin to respond differently to you—not only verbally, but in their body language.

> Modeling good behavior as a couple helps children and teens feel safe and loved. When they grow up, they will have some of the tools necessary to mediate their own relationship conflicts.

Knowledge is power. But you would be wise to exercise caution when correcting other people about their manner of speaking. The last thing you want is a power struggle with someone who feels as though you're "p.c.ing" (politically correcting) them to death. So choose to live it and model it.

When it comes to conflict resolution, a couple must be willing to keep the lines of communication open with each other and (when possible) with their former spouses. Developing strategies like these to deal with problems becomes easier as time goes on and you have more experience navigating your family dynamic. Developing new skills is like bridge building over the rough terrain. You can build new bridges of conflict resolution! Who doesn't want to be heard and understood?

Modeling good behavior as a couple helps children and teens feel safe and loved. When they grow up, they will have some of the tools necessary to mediate their own relationship conflicts.

The Decision Matrix

I created this matrix on the following page as a visual aide to help you and/or your spouse clarify decisions you need to make which affect your family. It is a tool that allows you to identify what the issue is, who it involves, and what motivation is behind it. Due to the extra members in the stepfamily, decision making is often more complex than in first marriages.

DECISION MATRIX

ISSUE _____

	Short/ Long Term	What is the Motive?	Who will be Affected?	Will this Heal or Hurt?	Driven from the Past?
Child					
Teen					
Young Adult					
Adult Child					
Step Parent					
Self					
Other Siblings					
Step Siblings					
The Child					
Spouse					
Former Spouse					
Extended Family					

Decision Matrix Questions

1. Determine the issue.
2. Will this issue be a short or long term situation? For example: Should we let Suzie join the softball league?
3. What is the motive behind this possible decision? For example: to help Suzy get exercise and engage in a more social setting rather than isolated up in her room.
4. Who will be affected? Who will get Suzy to practice? How expensive will this be? Will her other parent be able to assist in the cost?
5. Will this decision be a healing opportunity for Suzy? Could it help her to grow? Even if she is resistant, could it potentially help her?
6. Is this decision driven by a difficult time in my past or the past of the other person involved?

Stepping Stone — Resentments, Regrets, and Appreciation Exercise

I worked in a psychiatric facility in the late 1980s and early 1990s. My job was to run Family Week in an addiction unit, which focused on educating families about addiction and the role family dynamics play in the addiction cycle.

We taught family members how to use the Resentments, Regrets, and Appreciation Exercise so they could share their experiences with their loved one who was in treatment.

The beauty of this exercise was it is short, concise, and above all, respectful. It allowed family members to share a hurtful incident and also any regrets they may have had about the way the incident was handled.

The rules were as follows: each resentment, regret, or appreciation could only be two sentences.

The first sentence was a statement.

The second sentence was an I feel statement.

"I resent the day we were at the beach on July 4, 2015, and we fought over where to park the car and the kids were crying. I felt scared, overwhelmed, and unheard."

"I regret I did not speak up and insist we talk about this outside the truck where the kids couldn't hear. I feel sad, weak and disappointed in myself when I think back on how I failed to intervene."

"I appreciate how you spoke with our family counselor about this and are learning new conflict resolution techniques. I feel hopeful about our future."

I teach this technique to couples because it helps to clear the air in a loving, respectful manner.

The Resentments, Regrets, and Appreciation exercise is a healthy way to confront your spouse while also owning your part in an issue. It is also another technique you can practice in your journal if your spouse is unwilling to participate.

I hope you see you have wonderful tools to help you and your loved ones work through conflict. Communication is vital in any marriage, but especially a stepfamily marriage. Conflicts can escalate much faster in a stepfamily marriage because more people (and more fears) are involved. It is easy to let things slip by and not address them, leaving unresolved hurt and confusion to poison the family well.

Don't stop talking. It is of utmost importance to keep talking to each other. Just make sure you aren't waiting to have tough discussions until late at night when both of you are exhausted. As your marriage and children continue on the pathway, there will be many twists and turns. The adults change and grow. Kids do, too. New issues will emerge and old ones resurface, which will then need to be sifted through again.

Make sure you have regular time together where you can talk about things that are fun—future vacations, perhaps, or a dream you share of retiring. Dates should not be spent talking about kids and problems, don't you agree? You were people once before you were parents. It's always a good thing to remember that.

The Reporter Technique

When dealing with an ex-spouse, even one you get along with relatively well, stay calm, stay factual, and keep your interaction focused on the kids. Do not get caught up in the other parent's emotions. Think Spock from "Star Trek," not the ever-volatile Captain Kirk.

To use another example: when TV reporters are called to a warehouse fire, they never run into the burning warehouse. They maintain a safe distance emotionally and physically. They make sure they have the correct information before reporting the story.

You need to do the same. Stay calm and keep your tone neutral. If you can't make any headway, get off the phone or leave the situation by saying you have somewhere else to be. Try again later when the person is calmer.

In stepfamilies, conflicts will arise as children sort through their emotions and experiences. Much of what they are dealing with concerning the stepfamily—the divorce of parents or the death of a parent—goes unnoticed by their caregivers because it isn't immediately obvious.

When it becomes necessary to discuss your stepchildren with your spouse, you should do so with as little emotion as possible. If you have children of your own, you know how hard it is to hear from a teacher that your child misbehaved. Likewise, it is hard for your spouse to hear negatives from you about his or her children's or teens' behavior. Proceed in a gentle manner, and just share the facts. Then give your spouse time to take it in.

Children seem to have radar when it comes to picking the worst time to ask a complicated question. Prepare in advance. That way, you won't get caught off-guard. Resist the temptation to make snide remarks about your former spouse or bad-mouth them in any way. This creates terrible anguish within the child, for he or she is half of the person you're belittling. If mom or dad is a bad person, doesn't that make them a bad person, too?

———•◆•———

Stepping Stones for Listening and Reflecting

Fascinating research has been done on the differing communication styles of women versus men. What I'm about to say is a generalization (to which there are always exceptions), but as a rule, the reason men talk is to convey information. The reason women talk is to build rapport.

Men who are having conversations tend to be status seeking. Listening places them in a subordinate position, which is why listening can often be hard for some men. Speaking gives them the opportunity to jockey for status—to "one up" each other. Also, men tend to be solution oriented and may want to solve the problem.

Women's conversations tend to be consensus building. Theirs often is a spirit of cooperation, not competition.

But they are quicker to pick up on subtext—everything a woman has decided you're not saying but actually mean. Subtext can include tone and volume of the voice, body language and facial expressions.

Researchers note only thirty percent of what we say to someone is actually heard. What we're really paying attention to are each other's nonverbal cues.

So what does this mean to you?

Husbands can become frustrated by communication that isn't direct and informational. Wives often grow disenchanted when their attempts to connect are met with stony silence, or a quick solution.

Let's look at how a listening and reflection exercise can assist stepfamilies on their journey.

The following exercise is deceptively simple and a technique I commonly use in therapy.

Stepping Stones for Listening

I ask one person to be the speaker and the other to be the listener.

The listener's job is to reflect back what the speaker is saying.

I ask the couple to start with a fairly mundane topic before we delve into something more challenging.

The rules are easy. The speaker uses no more than five or six sentences at a time, which allows the listener to keep up with what that person is saying.

Usually when someone is talking, we are too busy formulating a response to really listen. That's why this exercise works.

After the speaker says the sentences, the listener reflects back what they heard. They respond by asking, "Did I hear you correctly?' or "Is that what you said?"

Be sure that the speaker doesn't exceed his or her sentence limit. Again, keep it at five or six sentences. This "call-and-response" pattern allows both parties to feel heard and understood. And yes, I am frequently amazed at how effective it can be when we really listen.

> Family members often feel as though they are being heard for the first time without criticism, anger or judgment.

Couples are often astonished by what happens to their relationship when they speak their hearts. Entire families have broken down in tears when doing this exercise in my office. Family members often feel as though they are being heard for the first time without criticism, anger, or judgment.

Even if a couple or a family can't come to an agreement on an issue, being listened to can be very healing. Let's be realistic; agreement does not always happen.

If you can practice this with your spouse for as few as five minutes a day, you will be amazed by how much it can transform your communication. Start out with easy topics, such as "How was your day?" The better you get with softball questions, the better prepared you will be for the tougher ones.

If a subject is particularly touchy, try practicing in a coffee shop or other public place that will keep you from flying off the handle. We all tend to behave better in public.

Will This Heal?

My friend and counselor Buddy Scott created the following phrase:

> **Is what I'm about to say or do going to help or heal or hurt?**

Buddy gave this gift to me almost thirty-four years ago. He knew I struggled with sarcasm and hurtful words. This phrase got stuck in my head, and no longer could I justify my sarcastic comments.

You can also ask yourself this question when you journal.

This stepping stone will help you think before you speak. It will give you time to consider your ulterior motives, if there are any.

Questions for the Journey

1. When you were growing up, how did your family express anger and disagreement? How do you express anger and disagreement?

2. What did you learn about communication and conflict in your previous marriage(s) and significant relationships? How did you express anger and disagreement then?

3. What would you like to do better in your marriage, with your children and with your stepchildren?

4. What stepping stones are you already incorporating? Acknowledge this and affirm yourself!

5. Which stumbling stones are your identifying with?

6. Consider taking out one stumbling stone for now and incorporating a new stepping stone in its place.

7. Who in your life has been a great listener? What did/does it feel like to be heard by that person? How could you improve your listening skills?

———•◆•———

7

Stepping Stones for Adult Stepfamilies

Pursue some path, however narrow and crooked, in which you can walk with love and reverence.

—Henry David Thoreau

M arrying after your children are grown has its advantages. The couple can focus primarily on the marriage. People considering an all adult stepfamily marriage lament about having found an amazing second chance, but feel time is short. When children are grown, they usually have their own lives. This allows for more investment in the relationship, less energy on raising children like in stepfamilies with younger children and teens. This can mean fewer complications.

However, adult children whose parents have remarried are an important but under-researched demographic. I would like to take a quick moment to discuss these unique and surprising challenges. In truth, they aren't much different from the ones you might expect if the children were younger.

Adult children and stepchildren issues have many different faces, but they usually boil down to the same three things: loyalty conflicts, jealousy, and they may have an attachment to things remaining as they were.

Common Issues in the All Adult Stepfamily

1. An adult stepchild moving home and the stepparent openly or secretly rejecting that.

2. An adult child that is independent but grieving the loss of their parents' marriage. Some of these adults are embarrassed and shocked by the hurt feelings that come up, even if they are happy for the remarried parent.

3. Active dislike between the stepchild and stepparent that tends to erupt during periods of stress.

4. An adult stepchild asking for financial support and attempts made on behalf of that stepchild's biological parent to ensure that financial support is given regardless of the stepparent's feelings on the subject.

5. An adult stepchild refusing to leave home and how this puts pressure on the biological parent/ stepparent relationship.

6. An adult child with ongoing financial or emotional problems.

We tend to forget stepfamilies don't always form when the children are young. Some form after the death of a spouse or a late-in-life divorce.

Odd as it seems, stepparenting an adult stepfamily can be just as challenging as stepparenting a younger one.

Some parents assume adult children will be fine with the new situation because they've started families of their own. It's true some adult children are delighted their parent is experiencing a second chance at love. In my practice, I have heard amazing stories of adult children welcoming a new spouse.

Unfortunately, some adult children (at least from the perspective of their parents) end up behaving poorly. Some of these adult children are surprised by their own hurt, negative feelings about a parent's remarriage.

Whether death or divorce is the basis for a remarriage, loyalty issues can arise in the hearts and minds of adult children. Fear of being replaced is not uncommon. So is jealousy. And for adult children who remember from their own childhoods a parent's second or even third marriage, emotions can resurface that are far from pleasant.

Some clients I've worked with felt no need to connect with parents or new stepfamilies. For adult children whose parents remarried multiple times, there was usually skepticism about how long a marriage would last, which made them reluctant to invest in any stepfamily relationship.

Part of the problem is adult children have a greater sentimental attachment to the status quo. There is also a long family history to safeguard. A thirty or forty-year marriage is a significant amount of time. These adult children want things to remain safe and comfortable—even if they have their own lives, their own concerns, or live halfway across the country.

But other adults, particularly those who lose a parent to death, often feel left behind as their surviving parent enters this new phase in his or her life. They see it as a personal affront to the deceased parent when family photos begin disappearing off the walls.

Adult children can walk into their old home, the one they grew up in, only to find it stripped of any link to the past, which may bring up new feelings of grief.

In some instances, private conversations with the parent in question are difficult to have because that parent wants to avoid any possible perception of disloyalty to the new spouse. Just like stepfamilies with younger children, parents may be thrilled to have a second chance, even if their children don't necessarily share their enthusiasm.

Stepparents tend to fall within one of two categories: those who jump in and embrace the family at hand, and those who retreat when they find their efforts to connect aren't being reciprocated.

Unfortunately, the world perceives stepparents as constitutionally incapable of loving their stepchildren. While it's true that deep bonds don't always happen in every stepfamily, a great fondness and love can occur, especially when the stepfamily is formed while the children are young.

Take the case of one of my clients, Susan, who keenly felt the responsibility of having to measure up as a stepmother.

Susan married when she was twenty-six-years-old and her husband, Doug, was in his mid-forties. Soon after they married, Doug gained full custody of his two children who were in their early teens at the time.

Determined to love Doug's children as her own, Susan set out to take their mother's place and give them a mother's love. She and Doug had one child together. A few years later, they had another.

When Doug's ex-wife came around, she consistently undermined Susan's attempts to parent. The stepchildren felt conflicted. Their mother insisted that since Susan had two children of her own now, they were being neglected—accusations that were as unkind as they were untrue, especially since Doug's volatile ex-wife was never going to win any Mother-of-the-Year awards.

But the damage was done. Although Susan tried for years to love and care for all the children, one stepchild ultimately decided to turn her back on the family. There were many issues, not just the stepfamily, but the rejection continues to haunt Susan to this day.

Now the grandmother of several grandchildren, Susan says there is still some tension within the family. Her goal is to make her peace with what she rightly calls the "is-ness" of her situation. It is important to note that sometimes these issues are never resolved, and the best anyone can do is to alter her perceptions rather than attempting to alter her circumstances. Susan is determined not only to accept the reality, but to grow and heal through it.

.

———————

The Importance of Timing

Despite cultural stereotypes, widows or widowers who remarry rarely see the new partner as a replacement for the previous one.

Remarried widows and widowers, on average, maintain a deep love for their original spouses. They tend to cite the longevity of their first marriage and their shared commitment to raising a family as the primary reasons for that deep and continuing bond.

> Marrying after your children are grown has its advantages. The couple can focus primarily on the marriage.

If a parent remarries in what the children consider to be "indecent haste," those children often struggle longer to accept the parent's new partner.

But there's another key issue and it seems to be a far touchier one among adult children: the importance of a new spouse knowing his or her place.

If a new spouse overreaches, either out of a sense of wanting to connect with the new family or possible nervousness about fitting in, adult children and stepchildren may be quick to find fault with that spouse. One example of that would be a new stepmother jockeying for a place in her stepdaughter's wedding.

For many adult children, having parents with multiple marriages leads to a sense of self-protectiveness. Most decide—whether consciously or not—that they would not make an investment in a new stepparent, seeing as how they revolve like a subway turnstile. There is a marked unwillingness to bother connecting with anyone who may or may not be in their lives or their children's lives over the long haul.

If both parents are remarried, especially to spouses the children find disagreeable, sometimes forfeiting a close relationship with either parent is preferable to the insincerity required to "keep up appearances."

Some of these adult children are surprised by their own hurt, negative feelings about a parent's remarriage.

Yet to what degree should the feelings of adult children and stepchildren even be considered? If adult children are busy raising families of their own, how much authority should they be given to dictate the terms and conditions of their parents' lives? At what point does any parent get to say: Enough. This is my life. I'll do with it what I want.

As both a therapist and an observer of family dynamics, I would say that a different set of rules applies to each family.

What's essential for adult children to remember is that at some point, parents are no longer just parents. They are people, like you. People who are entitled to live their own lives on their own terms with a partner who brings them joy and happiness.

Accepting this requires maturity and wisdom.

Not only is it important for you to exercise empathy toward your parent and his or her chosen partner, regardless of what your opinion of that partner may be, the same empathy should be shown to you as well. That doesn't always happen, especially in high-conflict families where emotional leftovers haven't been fully dealt with.

It may be true that "you were there first," but it is equally true the new partner is there now. You can't control how other people choose to behave. However, you can control how you proceed from this point forward.

For the sake of all involved, a new spouse must learn to be sensitive to the limitations of his or her role within the family. This means refraining from giving advice, taking sides, or offering an opinion. It also pays to remember there was a great deal of history prior to you. These things take time, just as with younger stepfamilies.

And it's way harder than new spouses think it will be, especially when they find themselves tempted to "form alliances" with those family members who seem the least threatened by the fact that they exist.

But when it comes to family politics, it pays to take the long view.

But when it comes to family politics, it pays to take the long view.

Being a new stepparent requires great diplomacy.

If there are exes in the picture, and those exes are openly critical of the new spouse, adult children may be listening to this criticism, too. Those exes who have not healed or moved on can create havoc even years after a divorce by insisting on their adult children's loyalty. Some adult children will try not to make waves by indulging the parent. I have seen cases, however, where the children never forgot how a parent destroyed their family. They may have forgiven, but never felt they could trust the parent who betrayed them.

Remember there is nothing you can do about other people's opinions of you. Proceed with love and dignity and let your new family catch up if and when it's ready.

How Long Will This Take?

When it comes to seeing the fruits of your labor, a consensus opinion among long term, successful stepfamilies is five to seven years.

During those years and after, mistakes will be made. There are no exceptions.

> The word step seems to fade away when you're in the grandparent stage.

But it's also good to remember despite the hardships, stepfamilies can and do work.

My husband and I are in the grandparent phase of our thirty-three-year marriage, and I am happy to report that grandparenting is far easier and more enjoyable than actual parenting. The word step seems to fade away when you're in the grandparent stage. There are no distinctions made between blood relations and steps.

Did it take years of effort to achieve this equilibrium? Yes.

Are there any guarantees? No.

Are there going to be times when the best thing you can do is go for a long walk to clear your head? Yes.

Are there going to be times you think you will never find your way? A hundred times yes.

If we consider the fact parenting is one of the hardest and yet most rewarding things we are called upon to do in this life, then stepparenting will test our character in ways we cannot imagine. Yes, allowances must be made for differences of temperament and experiences within the stepfamily, but there is only so much you can do to foster good feeling. The rest of it takes time and patience.

It is my hope to give you the benefit of advice from people who've been there, including myself.

Janet Nicholas

Investing in the Future

My client David is a prime example of someone who stuck with it. A tech recruiter, David was twenty-five when he married his older spouse, Joan, who had a college-age daughter from a previous marriage. His stepdaughter, Sasha, wasn't that much younger, which made it impossible for her to respect him as an authority figure or as a stepparent. There was little open warfare; rather, David and Sasha each lapsed into a state of quiet but seething resentment during the summers they shared a roof.

Young and immature himself, David made no attempt to bridge the divide or reach out to Joan's sensitive, artistic, and rebellious daughter. It wasn't that he was unwilling. It was more he didn't have the tools or the wisdom to do so.

Consequently, Sasha learned little was to be gained by staying close to her family. She moved out of state and stayed out of state until starting a family of her own.

Fast forward twenty years and both David and Sasha were different people. Sasha had a boy and a girl at this point, both under the age of five, and David found he enjoyed having the opportunity to grandparent her young children.

His participation in the lives of Sasha's kids brought him and Sasha closer together, too. Their old wariness never completely left, but their dialogue expanded and real affection took root. Sasha appreciated David's help, and David appreciated having her kids in his life.

> Their old wariness never completely left, but their dialogue expanded and real affection took root.

Don't forget it took over twenty years for this to happen. Before then, there had been a lot of mutual suspicion and studied avoidance.

On her part, Joan had never been able to identify what was wrong with Sasha and David's relationship. After a while, she just gave up and tried to do what a lot of people in her position do—pretend there wasn't a problem.

As anyone who has been in this situation will tell you, there is a fine line between being proactive about communication and being in denial. Accepting the kind of aloof politeness that tries to pass itself off as "getting along okay" is never going to be enough.

If you keep sweeping dust under the carpet, what happens? Eventually you get a big pile of dust that creates a lump under the carpet. One wrong step and all that dust goes poof, right out the sides.

Money

In adult stepfamilies, there's no tension like the tension around the issue of money.

If there is money to inherit, some adult children see the new stepparent as a threat to their inheritance. If you can, explain to them what your plans are and then formalize legally without allowing yourself to become offended by your children's justifiable concerns. Putting their fears to rest on this issue will go a long way toward making them feel comfortable with your new spouse.

It may take a long time before adult children open their hearts to the new partner in your life. If you're the biological parent, make it clear from the start that while you cannot force them to love this new person, you do expect them to act in kind and respectful ways. But recall respect works both ways.

Resist the urge to withdraw in hurt or anger if they fail to do as you wish. Challenges are likely to happen, at least in the beginning. Remember this new relationship may bring up grief or may even be a result of a phenomenon called The Sleeper Effect mentioned earlier in the book.

It is a generalization, yes, but for various reasons a lot of men are not good at building or maintaining relationships. And in a delightful twist of fate, it is often the stepmothers of adult children who keep those connections going and who develop a connection with their husband's children.

Finally, for parents whose adult children are having a hard time with a remarriage, be sure to remind them that as an adult, you have legitimate needs and desires which include having a life partner. Doing so doesn't have to diminish your relationship with them or minimize the importance of the previous parent.

Questions for the Journey

1. How would you describe the health of your stepfamily? Do you have areas of concern? In other words, if we were sitting together in a room how would you describe these concerns?

2. If you are having problems or sense you could improve your relationship with one or several members of your biological or stepfamily, write a letter to them you have no intention of letting them see. Vent. Explore your emotions. Then tear it up.

3. How do you see you and your spouse navigating the concerns in your all-adult stepfamily?

4. Now, write a letter from them to you. What would they say to you about the way they perceive your behavior? This is quite a bit trickier. But it is the first and perhaps biggest step toward exercising that most essential of the essentials, which is empathy. If you can empathize with another person

enough to take their position on an issue and see that issue through their eyes, you have mastered a skill which will serve you all your life, not just in this specific instance.

5. If after years of trying, you still find it impossible to love your stepchild or stepparent, list ten things you can at least appreciate about them. The list might look something like this: "I do not love my stepdaughter, but I appreciate the fact that when she's here, she is respectful to my own children." Being honest with yourself is important, and sometimes it can free you up to stop feeling ashamed or guilty about not feeling more loving toward someone. But it is also important to remind yourself what there is to like about that person. If we obsess over negatives all the time, we make it impossible for ourselves to ever be happy.

6. As the father in an adult stepfamily, how are you at reaching out to your children and their family (daughter or son-in-law, grandchildren)? Would you say your level of involvement has changed or stayed the same since your remarriage?

7. As the stepmother or stepfather in your stepfamily, how would you define your role?

8. If you have disappointments or frustrations in your stepfamily, what are you doing to deal with them?

———•◦•———

Stepping Stones for Stepfathers

We all want progress, but if you are on the wrong road, progress means doing an about-turn and walking back to the right road; in that case, the man who turns back soonest is the most progressive.

—C. S. Lewis

There is no road map for being a stepfather.

All too often, there's no award ceremony, either. Maybe we should start one!

But there are rewards that will eventually go to those who are patient enough to wait for them. Parenting a stepchild can be an amazing opportunity to impact a child's life.

> There is no road map for being a stepfather.

Because women are usually awarded custody of their children, it often falls upon the new husband to learn how to navigate the water. Conflicts over discipline are one reason second marriages typically stumble.

So what can a wise determined stepfather do to stem the tide? There are plenty of success stories, too. What can be learned from them?

———•◆•———

Stepfathers Who Have No Children of Their Own

John was a conscientious man of Southern upbringing, polite and reserved, but always willing to go the extra mile for his friends and family. When he met Brittany, it was love at first sight. "We joke about conducting our relationship in the elevator at work, which is how we met, actually," he said. "I'd seen her there for probably six months before I had the nerve to ask her out."

Brittany had two sons from her first marriage: Benjamin, who was twelve, and Jake, who was sixteen. Their biological father wasn't around much and successfully hid his money, which meant Brittany didn't receive as much child support as she was due. This caused hardship before and during her remarriage.

When John married Brittany and started living at her house, problems with the older son, Jake, became immediately apparent. "He made it really clear that he wanted nothing to do with me," John reported. "And I didn't have enough experience at the time to recognize that this was pretty typical teenage behavior. I took every rude thing he did personally and then blamed Brittany for not disciplining him better.

"I felt like an outsider in my own home. Here I was providing full support for kids that weren't even my own and instead of a tiny bit of gratitude, all I got was lip. Looking back on those first couple of years, it's a wonder I didn't lose it with that kid."

The marriage took a seismic hit as well. As John explained it, "Every time I raised my voice to Jake, Brittany would rush to defend him. I felt double crossed. I even moved out for six weeks one time because it was starting to affect my job.

"All I know for certain is that if the relationship with the kids doesn't work, the marriage can suffer. It took every ounce of compassion I had for Jake's disappointment in his own father and his inability to accept authority from any man just to make it through those first years. I also began to realize how much Jake was hurting. My being a responsible stepdad probably reminded him of what a disappointment his own had been so far. We also got counseling, which helped me define my role within the family. I can say with one hundred percent certainty that counseling saved my marriage."

As a therapist, I see this dynamic played out over and over again.

In the beginning of a remarriage, stepdads would be well-advised to not intervene too often. Research bears this out. It takes time and emotional investment to build the relationship with your stepchild.

It takes time and emotional investment to build the relationship with your stepchild.

Adolescence is a time of great turbulence and authority-challenging behavior anyway. Whether the family is a stepfamily or an original one, parents can expect a fair amount of hostility from their teens.

Sometimes, however, remarriages don't survive. My client Bill had been married for almost ten years to a tender-hearted woman named Yvette. Bill had no children of his own, but he did help raise his six-year-old stepdaughter, Suzanne.

Bill may have had a gruff exterior, but it hid a kind heart. He felt not having had children left him at a disadvantage because he had no way of understanding the intense, even exclusionary, loyalty between a mother and child. He didn't know how to reach out or what to do. And nothing could have prepared him for the impenetrable bond between Yvette and her daughter, Suzanne.

Yvette and Suzanne went out to eat dinner about three times a week and would never invite him. There was never even a question of inviting him. It hurt, and Bill started feeling like an outsider.

Yvette and Suzanne had their routine and he wasn't allowed to participate. Bill got tired of it after a while.

Then Yvette's brother got terminally ill and died. Bill was crushed. He'd loved the brother, too, and he had been a big part of their lives.

Bill understood his wife was undergoing a great deal of stress, but for him, the damage was done. They muddled through for a few more years until Yvette packed up her daughter and left.

After ten years, he is still grieving the loss of those relationships.

1. Know going in there are going to be stressors: time, money, work, past childhood baggage, old habits, your new spouse's expectations, and your own expectations. These things will conspire to make you crazy. Solution: As a couple, carve out as much time every week that is as cell-phone-free and TV-free as possible. Dinner, for instance. Time permitting, try to sit down together and talk. Avoid discussions, negative or positive, that focus on just one child. Think—equal time for everybody.

2. Stay connected to your spouse. She's why you're in this stepfamily in the first place. Keep those channels of communication open and try not to let any date nights or time spent together as a couple fall by the wayside. Reschedule if you must, but keep the date.

3. Know you're going to feel like you're on the outside looking in occasionally, especially in the early stages. If you know your reaction is a "healthy, normal" one, you will be less apt to panic and start blaming your wife or your stepchildren for any sense of isolation. Solution: talk to your wife about

it in private. You don't have to solve the problem right away. But unless you explain there is a problem, she can't read your mind and she can't help.

4. Offer to pitch in and help with the kids in whatever ways you can. Driving them to school, for instance, is a terrific way to add just the right amount of you into the equation in a safe, consistent manner. If the kids are younger, you can read bedtime stories or help with homework. Or you could pick up their favorite drink on your way home, offer to run them to the store for those forgotten school project supplies, walk the dog with them, or watch sports together if yours is a sports-minded stepchild.

5. Remember you will need patience, and never be afraid to ask for help. There is no shame in getting counseling from a psychologist, psychiatrist, or mental health professional. If you make your own mental health a priority, guess what? Everyone benefits, including your family.

6. Sometimes during the stepfathering process, your own "dark moments of the soul" can bubble up. The best way to deal with them is to ask for guidance. No one expects you to manage all this on your own.

Stepfathers Who Have Children

The good news? Any stepdad with previous parenting experience is already better qualified to handle the stress of the job.

The bad news? Not even previous parenting experience can prepare you for how difficult it will be to take a back seat when it comes to disciplining your stepchildren.

Experts agree a stepfather bringing his own kids into remarriage with a woman who already has kids is one of the toughest rows to hoe. But if it works, it can also be one of the most rewarding.

Trying to force the issue will not make it work. If anything, it will probably impede your progress. A child who feels forced to do something they don't want to do will typically resist your efforts at bonding or will fake bonding to please the grownups.

> Be flexible and avoid rigidity. Keep looking for what works and what doesn't.

So what can you expect?

Conflict — These can be conflicts between stepsiblings or conflicts between you and your spouse; many will likely center on the kids or disciplining the kids. Know going in these differences of opinion are natural, normal and par for the course. They don't have to derail your relationship unless you let them. Keep reviewing the parenting issues with your spouse. Be flexible and avoid rigidity. Keep looking for what works and what doesn't.

Sibling Jealousy — Despite your best efforts, someone is going to feel short-changed. The accusation of preferential treatment is sometimes justified. No matter how equally we try to treat our children, steps or otherwise, mistakes will be made. Your job is to try to diffuse explosive situations when they come up, to listen (without being defensive) if a child comes to you with this or any other grievance, and to keep a watchful eye for any trouble that might be brewing. Look for positives and strengths in your stepchild or stepchildren. It can be hard on the others if your child is the gifted and talented one in the family and they're the ones struggling. Help each child find a way to shine.

Bonding Issues — I've urged patience before and I will do it again. Proceed with honor, fairness and dignity, by all means. But at the end of the day, whether you bond with a child or not is mostly out of your control. Factors such as the age of the child must be taken into consideration. Also, the child's previous experiences with father figures. Slowly goes. When it happens, it will probably happen when you're busy doing other things. Like the proverbial watched pot, the water tends to boil when you're off enjoying something else.

Behavioral Change — Trying to get your stepchildren to change a behavior will automatically make you the enemy. Most things you say or do may lead to resentment. They will also be quick to sniff out any hypocrisies (i.e., do you hold your own kids to the same standard?) So a good rule of thumb is to discipline your own kids and try to be the one who delivers glad tidings to your stepchildren. Keep in mind cultural differences in stepfamilies, whether emotional or physical, that can affect this rule of thumb. The same should go for your wife—let her address issues with her own kids but encourage her to be the "fun" parent with yours.

All too often I talk to stepdads who confess to having given up on having any relationship with their stepchild. Teens are typically more difficult to connect with. However, I have seen situations where a teen was so grateful to have a father figure in his or her life, there were few problems. Each stepfamily is different.

Qualities one might associate with our cultural expectations for masculinity (assertiveness, goal-orientation, the ability to "get to the bottom line") have no place in the delicate filament wires of a stepfamily. Instead, a man can rely on his more "feminine" side— listening, waiting, receptivity. These are good attributes to develop under any circumstances, but they will serve you particularly well in stepfamily relationships.

It helps to see a child as a child without the qualifying possessive pronoun. Not your child, a child. At some point in the story of every successful stepfamily, parents stop thinking in terms of "my kids/her kids" and simply see them as "our kids." This may be years down the road, but it's a potent perspective and one I strongly encourage you to explore.

When There Is a Mutual Child

I have seen stepchildren who were delighted when there was a new sibling.

When a mutual child comes along, often stepparents understand the bond their spouse has with their children on a whole new level. This baby can bring the stepfamily together on so many levels. A stepparent can relax knowing they have a child of their own they can parent with their spouse right from the beginning.

However, I have also seen the contrary, which is when siblings felt forgotten or abandoned.

Often, biological parents and stepparents are oblivious to the harm they do by trying to force older children to accept a younger one. Children may be asked to share a bedroom or to remain gracious when gifts and privileges are showered on the new child. This is especially tough on older kids who were born when their parents were less established. Now that the parents are more financially successful, it's hard for the older children to witness the contrast between their earlier lives and the far cushier life of a younger sibling. Older kids may have struggled through college but now they see the younger half-sibling getting everything they would have loved to have.

In one family I worked with, a new baby came along and the doting grandparents set up a college fund. The older stepchild had no such support in place. It is difficult to remain pure of heart when you see a new sibling being lavished with money and attention while you receive nothing.

One of the final points I would like to make here is the impact guilt has in most stepfamilies where kids from previous marriages are raised together, either on a daily basis or just the weekends.

My personal observation—based upon years of living and also working with clients—is no matter how much we do for our kids, we will always feel guilty.

We will always feel as though we could have done better, done more, been more available. This is just one of the many curiosities about parenting that none of us is really prepared for when we sign on. And there is no better incubator for guilt than a stepfamily where stressed parents can never give one hundred percent to anyone, not themselves, not their families, not each other.

Giving up on the idea of a perfect world and perfect parenting is, perhaps, one of the biggest favors we can do ourselves. Taking that kind of unreasonable pressure off contributes greatly to our happiness.

Residence of the Stepchild

Where children live as their primary residence impacts the role of the stepparent.

Most stepfamilies are composed of a woman who marries a child's stepfather, with the woman being the primary custodial parent.

However, the rise of joint custody agreements provides children with the opportunity to see both parents each week.

The positives to being full time stepparent include having more time to build a relationship, to develop new rituals and to learn old ones, and the freedom to create schedules.

The down side to full time stepparenting is that there is greater potential for conflict.

The husband and wife in the stepfamily have to determine how they will set up their household and how they will parent. It is best to discuss in as much detail as possible what this will look like.

Each stepfamily is different and has different needs. Be prepared to make adjustments and be flexible. How the children respond to new schedules and new rules will determine how well the plan is working.

Avoid making any new rules concerning the stepparent. Keep the rules more about the family in general. If there are teens in the home, ask their opinion and input. Take a couple of weeks to introduce these rules before enforcing consequences if the rules are not observed.

―――・・―――

Non-Residential Parenting and Stepparenting

Being a nonresidential stepparent means there is often less time to develop a relationship with the child. You're basically parenting part-time. This on-again, off-again dynamic can make things confusing for the stepparent, the stepchild, and even one's own children.

Studies show part-time stepmothers perceive their role as minimal or even non-existent. Those who feel they play a role in the stepfamily are often conflicted about that role's importance. They can and often do experience guilt over not doing more for their stepchildren or for not feeling closer to them. But it is vitally important non-residential parents and stepparents remain involved in their children's lives.

———————

Questions for the Journey

1. Define your role as a stepfather. How do you see yourself in your stepchild's life?

2. What if any differences are there in your relationship(s) with male or female stepchildren?

3. Have you seen your relationship evolve in a positive or negative way? Or do you feel stuck?

4. How do you feel you and your wife are connecting? Are you doing your part to keep date day or night consistent each week?

5. If you are a stepfather with children of your own, how do you deal with any loyalty conflicts you have with your children versus your stepchildren?

———————

Stepping Stones for Stepmothers

*When we deny our stories, they define us. When we own
our stories, we get to write the ending.*

—Brene Brown, PhD LMSW

E mily had a lot of pretty amazing things going for her—she was
funny and smart and self-aware—but five years and two kids
into her marriage with Matthew, his teenage daughters, Sarah
and Felicity, came to live with them.

"I knew right away that I was going to fail at all of it," Emily
told me during our first session. "The girls and I had gotten along
great before they started living with us. But the minute they moved
in, our lives were turned upside down. Sarah was dating a guy with
a drug problem and Felicity was cutting herself. I used to lay awake
at night having one panic attack after another because I knew there
wasn't enough of me to go around. I knew I couldn't be an adequate
parent to my toddler and my preschooler and have anything left over
for my husband and my stepdaughters. Consequently, I felt guilty for

wishing they weren't there and ashamed that I couldn't do more to help them when they were clearly suffering."

It didn't help that Matthew's job frequently took him out of town, which left Emily to raise her kids and Matthew's two daughters almost as a single parent. It never occurred to her how much pressure she was under until she received a misdiagnosis on a mammogram and for the better part of a week thought she might be dying. "My first kneejerk thought was, 'Well, at least I won't have to deal with this anymore.' That's when I knew I had a problem."

Emily finally reached out for help, which is how she found her way to my office. She was so ashamed of her feelings of failure, she'd been afraid to talk to anyone. Something as simple and truthful as me telling her everything that was happening was common to almost every stepfamily with teenagers was an eye-opening experience for Emily. "How did I not know this?" she said. "Why did I wait all this time before looking for help?"

But most people never consider the possibility their situation isn't unique to them until they've reached critical mass. Instead, they just live with the shame of thinking there is something wrong with them and their failure is a sad testament to their own inadequacy.

Here were some of the things Emily discovered about herself and her stepfamily while we worked together.

1. Emily didn't have the same rights and privileges
    as her stepdaughters' mom, which also meant she
    didn't bear total responsibility for her stepdaugh-
    ters, either. "If anything happened, I always felt like
    that was on me," Emily said. "I had to learn that
    yes, I was their primary caregiver, but that didn't
    mean everything they did was my fault, even if
    their biological mom told me it was." She was also
    able to admit she struggled with loyalty and prefer-
    ential treatment towards her own children.

2. It pays to find a counselor or mental health professional up front, even if you don't feel like you need one. "Once I found out that everything I was experiencing was normal, it felt as though the heavens had parted and the angels wept. Just because I had occasional selfish thoughts didn't make me a selfish person."

3. The marriage must be held in a sacred space. "When Matthew and I drifted apart from each other emotionally, I didn't see it at first. Mostly, all I saw were the never-ending tasks ahead of me, all the things I needed to do for the family. Now, Matthew and I understand how important it is to make our relationship a priority while at the same time keeping a healthy balance of time with the kids. We know that investing in each other is what counts the most. Even if some things don't get done, that's okay so long as we have time together."

4. Try not to blame. "It doesn't do any good. Even if blame can be laid squarely at someone else's feet, so what? Blaming doesn't help. And in my head, I was blaming the kids for everything—problems with my marriage, my own stress and unhappiness. In the end, it doesn't matter whose fault it is. What matters is what you're going to do to solve the problem. Or, if the problem can't be solved or isn't yours to fix in the first place, what matters is adjusting your own attitudes about the situation so it isn't eating you up inside."

5. Wicked Stepmother Syndrome is real—at least in some stepchildren's eyes. "Any rules you try to enforce will make you seem like the stepmother from Cinderella," Emily told me. "I really needed Matthew to be at home more often so he could help. It meant taking a pay cut, but he got another job, one that enabled him to stay in town. I can't tell you what a difference it has made. Now he and I discuss what our 'must haves' are from the girls and Matthew fights those battles by himself. I support him at a distance, but don't chime in during these discussions unless asked. We rehearse before we sit down with the girls on issues that involve me. I can be there for them emotionally and physically and I am. But I don't have to argue with them anymore. I built a healthy emotional boundary."

6. Kids are kids. "My job is to set the example and to behave like an adult. Their job is to try to push my buttons. Now that I know this, I can expect it. Their behavior doesn't throw me for a loop anymore. I may fail from time to time, but I strive to be a role model to all the kids."

7. If something goes wrong, don't bury it. "I was a notorious burier of anger and resentment. Part of me felt as though I had no right to be angry and resentful. Now Matthew knows how important it is to just listen to me vent without interrupting or taking responsibility or trying to fix it. He just listens. When he listens, I feel loved and understood. It has made a huge difference in our relationship."

8. If a child or teen is complaining about the step-mother to their father (or vice versa) these types of scenarios need to be handled carefully. If a biological parent is only discussing the issue with the child, the problem may never be resolved. For a variety of reasons, children may not want to discuss it with the stepparent. They may fear fallout, they may even be dishonest, or misunderstand a stepparent's actions or intentions. The biological parent may also be concerned about emotional fallout or how this will affect the marriage. If you do not feel you and your spouse can handle it alone, do not hesitate to meet with a professional counselor who can help you sort it out.

Stepmothers Who Don't Have Children

Cecilia came into my office a few years ago after marrying her husband, Frank, who was about eight years older and had two children from a previous marriage.

His ex-wife was a horrible role model. Due to negligence on the part of Frank's attorney, the divorce and custody agreement drawn up allowed the ex-wife to move both kids several hundred miles away to Corpus Christi.

Cecilia and Frank were devastated. She told me that it was the single worst day of their marriage.

What was so perplexing to them was the court had initially awarded them temporary custody. So they fought the ex-wife's decision to relocate the children and lost. The ex-wife moved them in with her new boyfriend who also had older teens.

"The only way we got through it was our faith," Cecilia says.

"We grew stronger for the experience. We had to lean on each other more. And now we have a whole new depth of intimacy.

"But we've held off on having children because we want there to be a large gap in ages between the children we will have and his children. Since they're being raised so differently, we don't want those negative influences brought into our home and affecting our kids.

"For me, the big wakeup call was realizing that they were not my kids. I had to remember they were being parented differently. Even Frank and I parent differently. Frank was spanked as a child. He did this with his kids and I was able to persuade him to try other disciplining methods first. Spanking could never be my primary method of discipline.

"Do I wish someone had told me not to have such unrealistic expectations? Yes! I thought the kids would be better behaved. Sure, Frank's ex-wife has been difficult, but I've heard horror stories far worse. So I'm grateful for that.

"But the rewards of stepparenting are enormous. I love saying prayers with them. I love seeing the positive impact we have on their lives. And I love it when they call me 'bonus mom.'

"My mom and stepdad get to play grandparents now and they love it even though I don't have children of my own yet."

In all my years of practice, it is rare for me to find a woman entering a stepfamily who didn't underestimate how difficult it would be. This, too, is normal.

It's important to consider the pressure a stepmother feels to fulfill a specific role within the family—and that's true whether she has biological children herself or comes into the relationship with a clean slate. Society expects women to do the emotional heavy lifting whether they work outside the home or within it. This sets the woman up for an impossible task and for feelings of failure when she doesn't accomplish what she set out to do, which is everything.

In all my years of practice, it is rare for me to find a woman entering a stepfamily who didn't underestimate how difficult it would be. This, too, is normal. Without previous experience with children, how can anyone know what to expect?

So it is with women, usually those who've enjoyed a high degree of independence and are career oriented, who fall in love with a man only to belatedly realize he has an entire five-piece luggage set he can't go anywhere without.

Stepping Stones for the Journey

- It's not about getting someone to love you. Know that it will take time to build trust and time to build a relationship. Find all you can which is positive about your stepchild and try to focus on that. Remember how kids may be grieving over the realization their parents will never be together. Fair or not, in a kid's mind, you could be seen as the culprit.

- Don't take it personally. If your efforts to connect are met with hostility, don't make the mistake of assuming this is a forever thing. Kids change. Feelings change. Chances are the rejection isn't personal (although it sure feels that way). Make yourself available to your stepchild but never ever push.

- If you find yourself getting a little green-eyed over the love your husband has for his child, seek counseling at once. Few human emotions are more painful than jealousy, and with the right help, you won't have to suffer unnecessarily. In the context of being a stepmother, jealousy can be a sign of unresolved childhood issues around feelings of loss, rejection, and competition for a parent's love.

- If you haven't gotten married yet but can't behave in a loving and respectful manner to his children, consider whether this is the partner for you. This is different from actually loving his children. Many times, when we go through the motions of loving someone, love does eventually show up. If you build a foundation of trust and respect, deeper emotions often follow, even to a degree that will be surprising to you.

- Remain humble in the face of what you don't know. We could all be a little less judgmental and a little more inclusive, but that is especially true of stepmothers who don't have previous experience raising a child. Too often we can become critical of the spouse's ex-wife or her laissez-faire parenting style. The temptation to say something negative about her, even in front of her child, can be great. Resist that temptation. No child benefits from hearing bad things said about a parent no matter how true those things may be. When you say negatives about a child's parent, you are saying negative things about the child who knows he or she is half the parent you may be disparaging.

- Don't shame or belittle your husband—not to his face, but especially not in front of his kids. Model the kind of relationship skills his children need to see and may not have had the opportunity to observe from the previous marriage. That doesn't mean pretending things are great when they clearly are not. It means discussing things calmly and rationally before they get out of hand. Modeling a healthy loving marriage may be one of the greatest gifts you could give your stepchildren.

Janet Nicholas

- Don't take on all the parenting duties yourself. Sometimes a father will forget his new wife is not his children's natural mother. He will let her assume more than her fair share of the parenting burden because she's a woman, he has convinced himself he's doing a good thing by letting her bond with the children, or he has simply gotten lazy. Remember you were a person before you became a stepmother. Schedule time for yourself, too. Even something as simple as going to the gym or having coffee with a friend can do wonders for your overall happiness and wellbeing.

- Know that in some cases, some children just cannot or will not accept a stepmother or stepfather. But considering the grief and loss and emotional baggage already discussed in this book, loyalty conflicts to another parent, wanting a parent all to themselves, or an unwillingness to share with a stepparent can be a few reasons why, for some, that connection with a stepparent may not happen.

- Don't feel bad if you're "not there yet." Love takes time. Lasting relationships take time. Trust takes time. Accept that the most you may ever be able to feel toward your stepchildren is mild affection. If you stop beating yourself up over perceived emotional deficiencies and start allowing yourself just to feel, chances are love might slip in there, too. It never will if you keep trying to force it. Or if you berate yourself for not feeling it faster.

- For all the same reasons, be willing to fail. Sometimes, a situation has to fall completely apart before we can even try putting it back together again. Relationships are like that, too. When tempers flare and harsh words are spoken, it may feel as though things are always going to be this awful. But things never stay the same. The wheel of life is always turning, and it is the wise woman who remembers that.

- With great pain comes great understanding. Work, family, and relationships—all three can bring us joy. All three can bring us pain. It is human nature to want to invite the first and avoid the other. But being a stepmom, while undoubtedly distressing at times, can be one of the most rewarding experiences you will ever have. The trick is to remain open to it. To welcome pain as a normal and expected outgrowth of intimacy. Don't assume if it hurts, it must be bad. Think of it more as exercise for your soul. If physical exercise sometimes hurts, soulful exercise hurts, too. But it makes us stronger. Better. More deeply compassionate. Never forget that.

- Residential versus Non-residential Stepmothers: Residential stepmothers are at an advantage in that they have more time with their stepchildren. There is more opportunity to build a relationship, but also more time for challenges to occur. Non-residential stepmothers may have less responsibility since they don't see their stepchildren full-time. The downside can be less time to build and bond those relationships. However, there may also be less opportunity for negative interactions. Also, as in Cecelia's case, she went from being a part-time, then full-time and finally a very removed stepmother after the children were moved over three hundred miles away.

- Mutual Child: Often when stepmothers have their own child, it is a wonderful shift towards the positive. Having your own child means you have more impact over how that child is raised. It is a joint venture with your spouse.

Questions for the Journey

1. How would you define your role in your stepfamily?

2. Have you had to redefine or change your role?

3. If you have children of your own, are you ever conflicted over how to be loyal to your own children while taking care of your stepchildren?

4. Have you been able to find ways to reach out to your step-children?

5. If your stepchild is limiting or not allowing a relationship, how are you dealing with this?

6. How do you feel you and your husband have addressed parenting issues?

7. How is the residence of your children and/or stepchildren affecting you?

8. What are you doing to create that sacred space for you and your spouse weekly?

9. Are you making time for self-care? If so, how? If not, write down some things you will commit to doing for yourself weekly. A little can go a long way. Consider what you might do on a larger scale twice a year such as a two-day get away or retreat.

Stepping Stones for Those Who Seek Counseling

Life is pure adventure, and the sooner we realize that, the quicker we will be able to treat life as art.

—Maya Angelou

I n the late 80s, as a newly licensed chemical dependency counselor, I made my professional bones at an adult addiction unit in a psychiatric facility in north Houston. It was a week dedicated to the families of those who had a loved one in treatment. We focused on educating the family about addiction and we gave them a safe place to share with their loved one how the addiction had affected them.

To watch my patients listening to how their addiction had impacted their families was painful, yes, but it was also riveting and powerful. The courage it takes for families to salvage themselves from wreckage left by addiction is nothing short of breathtaking.

Yet despite my powers of observation, I was never able to predict what would happen to married couples; whether they would stay together or go their separate ways. First marriages, second marriages, stepfamilies, original families—there was no pattern to follow, no big neon arrow pointing in one direction or the other.

As family week ended and I'd listened with a heavy heart to all the devastation in these couples' lives, I would often think to myself, there is absolutely no way that relationship is going to survive.

But then, years later, I would see some of those couples walking down the street, seemingly happy and still together. What a pleasant, and yes, humbling, surprise. I'd also run into former stepfamily clients at the grocery store. They would often tell me how many years they'd been married, which was code for "We made it!"

So it is with stepfamilies. I have seen insurmountable problems overcome by couples. I should know—I was half of one of those couples.

Almost seven years into my stepfamily marriage with my husband, we hit a sizable rough patch. For the longest time, it felt as though there would be no healing and no hope.

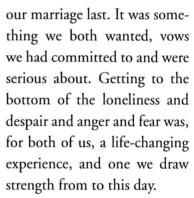

What I do know is this: if a marriage can survive a major storm, it can emerge from that storm stronger and better.

We worked hard to make our marriage last. It was something we both wanted, vows we had committed to and were serious about. Getting to the bottom of the loneliness and despair and anger and fear was, for both of us, a life-changing experience, and one we draw strength from to this day.

Here we are thirty-three years later, better for having climbed that mountain together.

I learned from my earliest days in counseling at that psychiatric facility no one can predict the future. No amount of experience or education can tell you ahead of the fact whether a couple will make it or not.

What I do know is this: if a marriage can survive a major storm, it can emerge from that storm stronger and better. My husband and I needed experts to help us navigate through the blinding fog and snow that had beset our marriage. We drew support from friends who had also made that journey. And we found a husband and wife counseling team to assist us through the disappointment, frustrations, misunderstandings, confusion, and pain. That counseling room was a sacred space for us to discuss things we could not share with anyone else, not even each other.

There are few places in today's hectic and media-saturated society that are truly private anymore. What a relief it was for us to share our hearts in their true pulpiness, nakedness, rawness. What a gift it is for anybody to be able to share in such a terrifyingly intimate way.

> I have seen insurmountable problems overcome by couples. I should know—I was half of one of those couples.

I am incredibly grateful to be in a position to pay that forward, to be there for my clients in the same way my counselors were there for me.

Stepfamilies need a place to be heard. The vast majority would benefit from direction and guidance.

By the time most of my clients arrive in my office, they are already in some form of crisis. Rare is the couple that seeks advice prior to the marriage. In the beginning of any relationship, when our eyes are blinkered by love, it is difficult to see that far down a dark and bumpy road.

If you wish to seek counseling, it is important to find a counselor or psychologist who has expertise in the area of stepfamilies. Some professionals in the mental health field aren't always attuned to the unique circumstances and needs of a stepfamily. Mistakes can be made. It always pays to find someone who knows their stuff.

It often happens that a child, preteen or teenager is the first one to start counseling and then parents and stepparents join later. But squeezing an entire family into family sessions can recreate all the same problems we're trying to fix—and magnify them. I find that it is best to meet with the couple first and then the children from each parent separately.

Trust is a huge issue with kids. Many times, I have children and stepchildren in my office who worry that what they say will get back to a stepparent or parent. It takes a long time to establish trust and to convince them that what is said in my office stays in my office.

When you find a counselor you think you can work with, I would encourage each person to make a list of the things of greatest concern to them. Attempt to put these concerns in order of importance. Your counselor will ask what has brought you to counseling and this will help you to organize your thoughts.

Some counselors will request an individual counseling session with each spouse after the first visit. This is my personal preference since it allows each person to talk to me privately. I find that couples beginning counseling are often fearful of offending one another, so the individual session is a good opportunity to get to the heart of what trouble is already brewing within in the relationship.

In addition to compiling a list of concerns about the relationship, I like for couples to make a list of strengths, too. This list gives a counselor more insight and direction on how to work with them and their stepfamily.

Not everyone is willing to go to counseling. Sometimes it may not be necessary or even recommended. So go by yourself. Do your work. The time and money you invest in you or your family will have rich rewards. It can make the difference between a family that stays together and a family that suffers the pain and anguish of another divorce. There are times when a previously unwilling spouse will see such a positive shift, they end up at my office, too.

Just as important, it can give you the opportunity to learn more about yourself—old programming that no longer serves you. Childhood trauma that continues to play a role in your adult relationships. Crippling trust issues. The better we know ourselves, the more available we can be for everyone else, including ourselves.

Contrary to popular belief, counseling isn't for the weak. Counseling is for the strong.

When a Stepfamily Marriage Ends

We cannot ignore those stepfamilies that do not survive the journey. Revisiting Shaunti Feldhahn's research statistics about remarriage reminds us that approximately thirty-one percent divorce in second marriages. Some couples may not be able to sort through all the past and its effects on the present. Some marriages are not able to withstand the multitude of issues such as children, parenting, money, and former spouses. Then, there are those who may have experienced abuse, addiction, mental illness, and/or life losses in their stepfamily. If your marriage did not survive, you must give yourself time to heal and sort through all that happened. I have counseled stepfamilies as they unraveled. A subsequent divorce is not for the faint-hearted. It is indeed beyond painful and discouraging. I encourage anyone facing divorce or who has been through the divorce of their stepfamily to find a good support group and personal counseling. It is vital to have support while going through this type of loss for you and your children.

Recommendations for Choosing a Counselor and for Premarital Counseling

I encourage everyone who seeks counseling to ask friends, a pastor, or physician for recommendations. Compile a list of several names and then call for an interview by phone. This will give you an idea about a mental health professional's areas of expertise, their methods of counseling, and their belief system. Some counselors like me have a more straightforward approach. Others tend to be more of a "listening" friend.

If you are thinking of getting married, I strongly urge you and your potential spouse to seek premarital counseling.

You both need to discuss your expectations for the marriage. What are you hoping to accomplish in this relationship? What will your division of labor be? How have each of you dealt with conflict resolution in the past? Would you like to change that in the future? What did you learn from your previous marriage which will help you in your new one? How are the children doing with the impending marriage? What are your former spouses like? How do you anticipate they will affect the marriage and parenting? What are your views on parenting?

One of the first things I do during a premarital counseling session is suggest the couple make one night per week a date night and their date night be a non-negotiable event. Children and problems are not to be talked of during date night. It is merely a time dedicated to enjoying each other's company.

Decisions about money must be made, and ideally this is done before a couple marries. Some people are spenders; other people are savers. Some will never be comfortable trying to live within a budget; others feel unloved if their wishes around the issue of money are ignored.

Money hardships can and often do happen when an ex-spouse fails to make child support payments. Jobs are lost. Extra kids mean extra expenses. Having a plan in place before these things happen is as important as having life insurance. In a way, it is life insurance. But both members of the couple have to agree to it. Being in a relationship never means "My way or the highway."

Sometimes we're so eager to put the past behind us and to cement a relationship (that will ideally keep us from having to be alone for the rest of our lives) we ignore the big red flags waving madly in our faces.

Even going on family outings together won't prepare you for what lies ahead.

Before a couple marries, future stepparents generally have limited contact with their future stepchildren. What contact they do have is usually that of a dinner guest—polite, friendly, and in no way potentially threatening. Then the couple moves in after the marriage and the stepfamily dynamics begin to unfold.

With even the smoothest transitions, a new stepparent moving into the house means everything changes. Most children struggle with any kind of change, even positive change.

I've worked with clients in premarital counseling sessions who have elected to go on family outings. During these outings, the children sometimes behaved rudely or aggressively toward the other children or the potential stepparent.

Believe it or not, they are doing you a favor. They are giving you a preview of things to come—

Believe it or not, they are doing you a favor. They are giving you a preview of things to come—and the opportunity to do something about them before those things become an even bigger issue in your marriage.

Consider matters from their perspective. Their lives have been drastically altered. Now an adult who does not necessarily love them—at least not yet—has moved in and is trying to exercise authority over their lives.

How would you feel if that were you?

Humans are adaptable. This is the thing that rightly gives us hope. Humans have proven time and again how adaptable they are. But sometimes, without counseling, it can be very difficult to provide that caregiving in a loving and consistent manner.

Last but not least, I would like to discuss potential problems with ex-spouses.

For an ex-spouse to be sincerely overjoyed that you have someone else in your life is rare almost to the point of absurdity.

Of course they're worried. Depending on the circumstances of your split, they may be downright bitter.

From their perspective, at least, some will think the choice of partner leaves a lot to be desired.

Or as is often the case, your ex simply isn't capable of wanting to see you happy. For some exes they may be worried about how your new spouse will affect their children.

Regardless of the reason, you may never have a high-functioning relationship with your ex. You may also marry someone who doesn't have a high-functioning relationship with their ex.

So where does that leave you?

When you marry someone, you aren't just marrying that person. You're marrying their kids, yes, but you're also marrying their extended family, their boss, their pets, and most importantly, you're marrying their ex-spouse.

Consider it a gift with purchase.

It's important that you know that going in. All too often someone will sit down in my office, scratch his head, and say, "I had no idea my wife's ex would be so vindictive."

Or "My husband's ex-wife resents any time I spend with his kids."

> **I want to applaud the exes who are reasonable and welcoming of the new stepparent.**

I want to applaud the exes who are reasonable and welcoming of the new stepparent. This is the best-case scenario when all parents can work together for the good of the children. It decreases confusion for the children, models healthy relationship behavior, and cuts down on chances the kids will be able to manipulate adults.

Know ahead of time what you're signing on for. This doesn't always or even usually translate into you leaving the relationship—rather that you go into it with open eyes, which will prevent you from being bitter and disillusioned later on.

Questions for the Journey

1. What's motivating your desire to get married? There's only one acceptable answer to that question and you already know what that is—love. If you love this person, warts and all, and still want to spend your life together, you are well on your way to a happy union. But if you are getting married because you're lonely or because you think no one else will have you, proceed with caution. That is not a strong enough foundation for any relationship, let alone one fraught with stepfamily peril.

2. Do you still have unresolved emotions towards your ex? This is more common than you think. If you weren't the one who put the kibosh on your previous relationship, there may be a whole raft of emotions you need to sort through before you're ready for a new one. Even if you were the one to end that relationship, you may still be experiencing some emotional baggage that needs more unpacking and sorting through.

3. You've seen this person at their best. But have you seen them at their worst, too? All too often, especially when we have kids and recognize the downside to dating someone with kids (making us feel even more "undesirable"), we jump into relationships we aren't yet prepared for. Three or four months in and we're already thinking about getting married. I'm here to tell you that you can't always trust your feelings. Until you've weathered a storm or two, until you've seen that person stressed out of his or her mind, you aren't ready to be married. Experiencing conflicts before marriage can be a positive. It's important to see how you and your fiancé deal with them.

4. What is this person's best quality? What is his/her worst? You may think the way your potential spouse shuts down emotionally when under fire is a welcome contrast to your former spouse's extreme volatility. But just wait till you can see there's a big problem but don't know what it is yet because your partner won't talk about it. In marriage and in life, it is often the "little" stuff that gets under our skin. Recognizing your irritation for what it is will keep you from blowing things out of proportion later on.

5. Where do you want to be ten years from now? Where does your potential spouse want to be ten years from now? If you're a teetotaler whose dream is to travel but your spouse has plans to eventually move back to his hometown and open a bar, you would be wise to take these different visions for the future into consideration. All too often we think we can change our partner's mind about things. Can people change? Yes, they can. But marrying someone based on the fact they will change is tricky at best. When you marry someone, you marry them as they are now. Accept the fact that you can't control anyone—nor should you. If a couple is to stay married, compatibility must extend beyond the next year or two.

----•◆•----

11

Stepping Stones for Relationship Building and Self-Care

Maps, road signs and a few useful phrases are good things, but infinitely better is Someone who has been there before and knows the way.

—Elisabeth Elliot

I'd been working with Robert and Mariana and their stepfamily for several years, including a period before they were married. One son was from her previous marriage, and one son and a daughter were from his.

They'd started out on shaky ground because Mariana's previous husband had not only abandoned his young family, he'd left them in ruinous debt due to his gambling addiction.

Not surprisingly, this had caused a huge rift between him and Mariana. Rather than hash out custody in court, Her ex-husband had simply saved his money for the video poker machines. He moved to a state where gambling was legal and severed all ties with her.

Their son, Alex, was the one who lost the real bet, of course. He had serious trust issues long before his stepfather Robert entered the picture.

But Robert was actually in a unique position to understand how Alex felt. His own father had been an alcoholic. When Robert was thirteen, his father ran off with a friend of Robert's mother, leaving her to raise Robert and his five siblings alone with no financial help.

Sometimes in life, our deepest wounds become our greatest gifts. Robert had been deeply wounded by his father's behavior. This created within him a steely determination to avoid those same mistakes. He'd committed himself body and soul to his first wife. When she cheated on him, he refused to leave and did everything he could to work things out.

Robert invested in his own recovery through his church. He committed to understanding the traits of an adult child of an alcoholic and how this might have been affecting his present day relationships. His recovery program gave him the roadmap he needed to heal and create a new path for his life.

But trust is a fragile thing and easily shattered. Eventually, she left him to raise their two children by himself.

Fast forward four years and this is where Robert and Mariana were when I first began working with them.

> Early on, they'd been wise enough to see that there were major relationship-ruining pot holes in the road ahead.

Early on, they'd been wise enough to see there were major relationship-ruining pot holes in the road ahead. Neither wanted to duplicate mistakes from the past. They came to me with great sincerity and an unmistakable desire to make things work. It was a good place to start.

Per my suggestion, both Robert and Mariana kept journals. Robert was resistant at first—a lot of men are in the beginning. He eventually became a more prolific "journalist" than Mariana. Journaling helped them articulate their hopes and fears. They also chronicled their victories and positive memories along the way.

We discussed their findings in my office. Mariana's son, Alex, a dyslexic, found the process of journaling to be tedious and frustrating, but Alex was blessed with the ability to express himself verbally, so we worked with that. It always pays to be flexible. Robert's children were younger and I used a variety of age-appropriate ways to encourage them to talk about their feelings, which were mostly ones of abandonment.

Once the air was cleared, we set about creating one of the most important aspects of successful stepfamily life—ritual. This doesn't have to be religious ritual, although it can be. Family ritual can be something as simple as every Friday night ordering a pizza and watching a movie together. Ritual can be having a snack after homework is done. Or doing yard work together every Saturday morning followed by a trip to the ice cream parlor.

Ritual, consistently performed, gives children structure. Structure helps children feel safe. Rituals create memories, which are well worn paths of familiarity that make us feel cared for. These sense memories can go deep and are a powerful tool.

> **Rituals create memories, which are well worn paths of familiarity that make us feel cared for.**

Have family meetings about where to go, what to do, how to do it. Try to make this as democratic a process as possible and with an eye toward making everyone feel as though their voice is heard. Be sure to keep those meetings brief! Rituals or traditions can be taken from the previous marriage or from your family of origin. But try to get every member of the family to chime in a few new rituals, too. It can take time for traditions grow roots, but they are worth the wait.

On Christmas Eve, maybe take the family ice skating. Or maybe you hop in the car and go look at all the twinkling holiday lights. A trip to the zoo could be a monthly event, especially if you have younger children. Fourth of July could be spent going to the same place every year to have a picnic and watch fireworks. Have a weekly tradition where everyone helps out preparing a meal and eating together.

Three things are important here.

1. Continue spending time with your biological children. One-on-one time. Family outings are family outings. They're for everybody. But have a few things that you do only with your biological children. Just as you are the parent who disciplines them, so too must you be the parent who spends special time with them. If there were things you did together before becoming part of a stepfamily, do what you can to continue that tradition.

2. Spend time doing things with each stepchild. Start small. If the stepchild isn't receptive at first, approach the situation from a different angle. Everyone has at least one thing they can't resist— in my case, it's chocolate chip cookies. Maybe you have a stepchild who also likes chocolate chip cookies. You could, perhaps, make them together. Baking is a terrific way to bond with anybody provided you don't become a tyrant in the kitchen. Or you could discover a bakery and make it your special place.

3. Create memories together as a family. Speaking of baking, here's a heartwarming story for you. A client of mine, Meghan, knew her stepdaughter loved to make brownies. Meghan had a great many talents; baking wasn't one of them. But

when Sylvie, her stepdaughter, asked if they could make some one night, Meghan agreed.

She went to the kitchen and turned on the oven. Unfortunately, Sylvie had put a green plastic ball in the oven some months before and then forgot about it. She'd done it to keep the ball away from the dog, which kept slobbering on it. At first, no one knew why acrid black smoke started billowing out of the oven, but Meghan panicked, tore the fire extinguisher out of the wall (and part of the wall with it), and then trained it on the blackened object inside her oven.

There weren't any brownies that night, but everyone—Meghan, Sylvie, Sylvie's father and all their friends and neighbors enjoyed a good laugh. What started out as a kitchen disaster has now become a favorite memory, one told and retold by the whole family. Such mishaps, when seen in a humorous light, are worth their weight in gold. Rituals and traditions make for terrific family "mishaps."

Time For You

Finding ways to reconnect to yourself is every bit as important as what you do for your family. Women in particular, have a difficult time giving themselves permission to "self-care." But even small gestures (a cup of coffee with a friend; a mani-pedi; an hour at the gym) can have big returns. For me, it's a walk through the woods and being out in nature.

> **We must find ways to keep our internal batteries charged.**
>
> ——•——

You won't have anything to give back if you don't take care of yourself, too, which is why I encourage men and women in the marriage to keep some time for each other, yes, but also time for themselves.

Think how a car battery functions. You can only run one car on one battery. Sure, you can jump start someone else's car on your battery, but that's about it. If you try to do any more than that, your battery will just keep running down until the car doesn't work anymore.

Humans operate along these same principles. We must find ways to keep our internal batteries charged. Define what this means to you. If you played racquetball once a week before your got married, be sure to keep playing racquetball after. Did you take Spanish lessons? Continue taking Spanish lessons. When our children were still living at home, I would sometimes get away for an overnight. A couple of times during the year I would go on a two-day retreat with dear friends. I always returned rejuvenated and with positive leftovers to share with my family. Husbands need this as well.

Of course, you must moderate what you want with the needs of your family, but as a member of that family, you're allowed to have needs, too. Ignoring them will inevitably lead to a lack of fulfillment and balance in your life—no matter how much you love your family.

——•——

From My Heart to Yours

It is my sincerest hope that the worries you had about your stepfamily, the worries that drew you to pick up this book in the first place, have been replaced by a growing sense of hope, a new sense of direction. I also hope you feel as though you have been validated in all the things you are doing well. There is nothing you are going through that hasn't already been gone through—and survived—by millions of stepfamilies. Draw strength from that.

There is one last story, from a distant past, I would like to share that has given me great strength. It is the story of Joshua leading his people, the twelve tribes of Israel, into the Promised Land. Theirs is an inspiring journey and one with many unexpected twists

> Things are taking place behind the scenes, upriver if you will, that we cannot always see.

and turns. Do you remember it? Joshua had been instructed by God to lead the Israelites across the Jordan River. Normally, this river was not formidable. But, the day they were to cross, it became a raging, flooding river. It seemed impassable—even treacherous. Joshua and his people stood at a distance and wondered how they would ever cross such a torrent.

But the instructions were clear: send twelve priests, one from each of the tribes, and have them wait by the river's edge. They knew not what they faced on the other side and they could not see what was happening. Out of their view and twenty miles upriver, the waters began to heap up in a pile. Eventually, the river's flow slowed and then ceased. The account says that they all crossed over on firm, dry ground. They passed from one land to another and one life to another, relying on their great faith.

Shepherding a step-family is a lot like Joshua's journey. The water is moving fast and at times it may look impossible to navigate. But as you stand on the banks of your stepfamily journey, you will begin to see that there is a time

> Choose a way to commemorate the stepping stones of success in your stepfamily journey.

to wait and a time to act. Things are taking place upriver—if you will—that we cannot always see, but they are happening in the hearts and minds of each adult and child in the stepfamily.

Stepfamilies just want a second chance. They want the opportunity to do things different this time. They want the opportunity to have a good marriage. And one more interesting detail about crossing the Jordan: The last instruction after they crossed over, was to return to the middle of that same river. What an odd thing! They were asked to pick up twelve stones to commemorate their journey. I hope you will consider doing the same. Choose a way to commemorate the stepping stones of success in your stepfamily journey. Celebrate the river crossings and be diligent to grieve the losses. Of course, there will be challenges along the way. That is the nature of life.

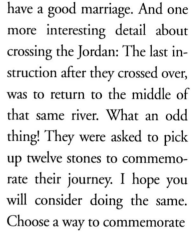

People are worth the investment of time—children especially. As a spouse, parent or stepparent, you are in a unique position to make the world a better place, one child at a time.

But you haven't been idle.

By reading this book, you have clearly demonstrated a willingness to learn what the pitfalls are so you can make things better—so you can make things work.

Now you know what it takes to have a healthy stepfamily—patience. Empathy. Diplomacy. Love. Oh, and did I mention patience?

Successful stepfamilies are successful because of parental teamwork. For any family to function well, adults must do more than their fair share of adulting. These demands are easily tripled when you merge families.

Throughout this book, I have sought to show you how to cultivate the skills you'll need in order to make a difference in your life, your spouse's life, and the lives of your children and stepchildren.

We are here on this planet to love others—even when there is no hope of reward. We love because we are human and they

About the Author

J anet Nicholas is a licensed professional counselor, chemical dependency counselor, and equine-assisted psychotherapist. Her professional practice is in The Woodlands, Texas. She has been counseling families and individuals since 1989.

In her spare time, she paints and rides horses with her husband of thirty-three years on their beautiful ranchette. As a counselor, wife, mother, stepmother and now grandmother, Janet has dedicated herself to the betterment of others and is lovingly characterized as someone who gives "straight talk from the heart."

Resources for the Journey

"Are Stepchildren at Higher Risk for Abuse Than Biological Children?" A Good-Therapy.org News Summary April 9, 2013.

Bray, James, and John Kelly. *Stepfamilies: Love, Marriage and Parenting in the First Decade.* NY: Broadway Books, 1999.

Browning, Scott, and Elise Artelt. *Stepfamily Therapy: A 10-step Clinical Approach.* 1st ed. Washington, D.C.: American Psychological Association, 2012.

Chambers, Oswald. *My Utmost for His Highest: An Updated Version in Today's Language.* Dodd, Mead & Co., 1935. Oswald Chambers Assoc., 1963. Ed. James Reimann. Discovery House, 2010.

Clawson, J., and L. Ganong. Need article title. *Journal of Family Nursing* 8 (1) (2002): 50-72.

Cloud, H., and H. Townsend. *Boundaries: When to Say Yes, How to Say No.* Grand Rapids, MI: Zondervan, 2002.

Crohn, H.M. "Five Styles of Positive Stepmothering from the Perspective of Young Adult Stepdaughters." *Journal of Divorce and Remarriage* 46 (2006): 119-134.

Elder, G. H., M. K. Johnson, and R. Crosnoe. "Emergence and Development of Life Course Theory." In *Handbook of the Life Course,* eds. J .T. Mortimer and M. J. Shanahan, 3-19. New York, NY: Kluwer Academic, 2003.

Elkind, David. *Child Development and Education: A Piagetian Perspective.* Oxford UP, 1976.

Elkind, David. *Children and Adolescents: Interpretive Essays on Jean Piaget.* Oxford UP, 1970.

Elliot, Elisabeth. *A Slow and Certain Light: Thoughts on the Guidance of God.* Waco, TX: Word Books, 1976.

Erera-Weatherly, P. "On Becoming a Stepparent: Factors Associated with the Adoption of Alternate Stepparenting Styles." *Journal of Divorce & Remarriage* 25 (1996): 155-174.

Everett, L.W. "Factors that Contribute to Satisfaction or Dissatisfaction in Stepfather-stepchild Relationships." *Perspectives in Psychiatric Care* 34 (2) (1998): 25-35.

Falci, C. "Non-resident Fathers' Relationships with Their Secondary School Age Children: Determinants and Children's Mental Health Outcomes." *Journal of Adolescence* 29 (4) (2006): 525-538.

Feldhahn, Shaunti. *The Good News About Marriage: Debunking Discouraging Myths about Marriage and Divorce.* Sisters, OR: Multnomah Books, 2014.

Finkelhorn, D., et al. "Victimization of Children and Youth: A Comprehensive National Survey." *Child Maltreatment: Journal of the American Professional Society on the Abuse of Children.* 10 (1) (2005): 5-25.

Fisher, Bruce, and Robert Albert. *Rebuilding When Your Relationship Ends.* 3rd ed. Oakland, CA: New Harbinger Publications, 1999.

Ganong, L.H., M. Coleman, and T. Jamison. "Patterns of Stepchild-Stepparent Relationship Development." *Journal of Marriage and Family* 73 (2) (2011): 396-413.

Gottman, John, and Julie Gottman. "Blog: An Introduction to Emotional Bids and Trust Entry." The Gottman Institute, 2012.

Hetherington, E.M. "An Overview of the Virginia Longitudinal Study of Divorce and Remarriage with a Focus on Early Adolescence." *Journal of Family Psychology* 7 (1993): 39-96.

Hetherington, E.M. "Family Functioning in Non-stepfamilies and Different Kinds of Stepfamilies: An Integration." Monographs of the Society for *Research in Child Development* 57 (2/3) (1999).

Hetherington, E.M. "The Influence of Conflict, Marital Problem Solving and Parenting on Children's Adjustment in Non-divorced, Divorced, and

Remarried Families." In *Families Count: Effects on Child and Adolescent Development,* eds A. Clarke-Stewart and J. Dunn. 203-237. NY: Cambridge UP, 2006.

Hetherington, E.J., and W.G. Clingempeel. "Coping with Marital Transitions: A Family Systems Perspective." *Monographs of the Society for Research in Child Development* 57 (2/3, Serial No. 227) (1992).

Instone-Brewer, David. *Divorce and Remarriage in the Church: Biblical Solutions for Pastoral Realities.* Il: Intervarsity Press, 2003.

Jones, A.C. "Transforming the Story: Narrative Applications to a Stepmother Support Group." *Families in Society: Journal of Contemporary Social Services* 85 (2004): 19-138.

Koren, C., and S. Lipman-Schiby. "Not a Replacement: Emotional Experiences and Practical Consequences of Second Couplehood Stepfamilies Constructed in Old Age." *Journal of Aging Studies* 31 (2014): 70-82.

Kreisman, Jerold J., and Hal Straus. *I Hate You Don't Leave Me: Understanding the Borderline Personality.* NY: Penguin Group, 2010.

Kubler-Ross, Elizabeth, and Ira Byock. *On Death and Dying: What the Dying Have to Teach Doctors, Nurses, Clergy, and Their Own Families.* Reprint. NY: Scribner, 2014.

Levin, I. (1997a). "Stepfamily as a Project." Marriage and Family Review 26: 123-133.

Levin, I. (1997b). "The Stepparent Role from a Gender Perspective." *Marriage and Family Review* 26: 177-190.

Levine, Peter A. *Waking the Tiger: Healing Trauma.* Berkeley, CA: North Atlantic Books, 1997.

Looney, Paul A. *Take It to the Cross for Couples: From Conflict to Connection.* Charleston, S.C.: Thrown Pot Press, 2016.

Marsiglio, W. *Stepdads: Stories of Love, Hope, and Repair.* Lanham, MD: Rowman & Littlefield, 2004.

Marsiglio, W. "When Stepfathers Claim Stepchildren: A Conceptual Analysis." *Journal of Marriage and the Family* 66 (2004): 22-39.

Martin, Wednesday. *Stepmonster: A New Look at Why Real Stepmothers Think, Feel, and Act the Way We Do.* NY: Houghton Mifflin Harcourt, 2009.

Noel-Miller, C.M. "Former Stepparent's Contact with Their Stepchildren After Midlife." *The Journals of Gerontology* Series B, 68 (3) (2013): 409-419.

O'Connor, T.G., E. M. Hetherington, and W. G. Clingempeel. "Systems and Bidirectional Influences in Families." *Journal of Social and Personal Relationships* 14(4) (1997): 491-504.

Orchard, Ann L., and Kenneth B. Solberg. "Expectations of the Stepmother's Role." *Journal of Divorce and Remarriage* 31 (1-2) (1991): 107-23.

Papernow, Patricia L. *Surviving and Thriving in Stepfamily Relationships: What Works and What Doesn't.* NY: Routledge, 2013.

Papernow, Patricia L. "Thickening the 'Middle Ground:' Dilemmas and Vulnerabilities of Remarried Couples." Psychotherapy: *Theory, Research, Practice, Training* 24 (35) (1987): 630-639.

Pennebaker, James. *Writing to Heal: A Guided Journal for Recovering from Trauma and Emotional Upheaval.* Oakland, CA: New Harbinger Publications, 2010.

Pryor, Jan. "Children in Stepfamilies: Relationships with Nonresidential Parents." In *The International Handbook of Stepfamilies: Policy and Practice in Legal, Research, and Clinical Environments,* Chapter 15. NJ: John Wiley & Sons, Inc., 2008.

Pryor, Jan. ed. *The International Handbook of Stepfamilies: Policy and Practice in Legal, Research and Clinical Environments.* NJ: John Wiley & Sons, Inc., 2008.

Ricci, Isolina M. *Mom's House, Dad's House: Making Two Homes for Your Child.* Rockefeller Center, NY: Fireside, 1997.

Scott, Buddy. Forgiveness Document. N.p., n.d.

Scott, R.A. "Buddy." *Relief for Hurting Parents: How to Fight for the Lives of Teenagers.* Rev. Lake Jackson, TX: Allon Publishing, 2004 & 2017.

Siegel, Daniel J. *Mindsight: The New Science of Personal Transformation.* NY: Random House, 2010.

Tannen, Deborah. *That's Not What I Meant: How Conversational Style Makes or Breaks Relationships.* Harper, 1987.

Tronick, Edward. "Still Face Experiment." www.youtube.com/watch?v=CZ8Tx1AEup4. July 7, 2013.

Vinick, B.H. and S. Lanspery. "Cinderella's Sequel: Stepmothers' Long-term Relationship with Adult Children. *Journal of Comparative Family Studies* 31 (2000): 377-384.

Wallerstein, Judith S., and Sandra Blakeslee. *Second Chances: Men, Women, and Children a Decade After Divorce.* NY: Houghton Mifflin Co., 1996.

Wallerstein, Judith S., Julia Lewis, and Sandra Blakeslee. *The Unexpected Legacy of Divorce: The 25 Year Landmark Study.* NY: Hyperion, 2000.

Waterman, B. "Doing to Being: Psychological Factors Influencing Women's Experiences of Stepmothering." Paper presented at the annual convention of the American Psychological Association, Psychoanalytic Division, San Francisco. August, 2001.

Weaver, S.E., and M. Coleman. "A Mothering but not a Mother Role: A Grounded Theory Study of the Nonresidential Stepmother Role." *Journal of Social and Personal Relationships.* 22 (2005): 477-497.

White, L., and J. G. Gilbreth. "When Children Have Two Fathers: Effects of Relationships with Stepfather and Noncustodial Fathers on Adolescent Outcomes." *Journal of Marriage and the Family* 63 (2001): 155-167.

Feeling Words

Loved	Appreciated	Hate	Degraded
Adored	Consoled	Unloved	Bashful
Idolized	Comforted	Loathing	Self-conscious
Enchanted	Secure	Despised	Shy
Ardor	Yearning	Listless	Uncomfortable
Infatuated	Popular	Moody	Embarrassed
Tender	Peaceful	Lethargic	Inhibited
Liked	Appealing	Gloomy	Humiliated
Cared for	Determined	Dismal	Alienated
Esteemed	Sure	Discontented	Puzzled
Affectionate	Attractive	Tired	Edgy
Friendly	Approved	Dejected	Upset
Regarded	Untroubled	Unhappy	Reluctant
Benevolent	Grateful	Bored	Timid
Alive	Elation	Bad	Mixed up
Vibrant	Enthusiastic	Forlorn	Baffled
Independent	Zealous	Disappointed	Confused
Capable	Delighted	Weary	Nervous
Happy	Eager	Frustrated	Tempted
Great	Optimistic	Sad	Tense
Proud	Joyful	Depressed	Worried
Gratified	Courageous	Sick	Perplexed
Excited	Hopeful	Disconsolate	Troubled
Patient	Pleased	Dissatisfied	Bewildered
Strong	Excited	Fatigued	Frightened
Good	Interested	Angry	Anxious
Inspired	Jolly	Hurt	Dismayed
Anticipation	Relieved	Miserable	Apprehensive
Anxious	Glad	Pain	Dreadful
Amused	Warm	Lonely	Shocked
Relaxed	Valiant	Exhausted	Panicky
Comfortable	\brave	Indifferent	Trapped
Content	Brilliant	Unsure	Horrified
Keen	Venturous	Impatient	Afraid
Amazed	Peaceful	Dependent	Scared
Sensitive	Intelligent	Unimportant	Terrified
Wanted	Daring	Regretful	Threatened
Worthy	Smart	Torn-up	Sullen
Pity	Unpopular	Inadequate	Provoked
Respected	Suspicious	Ineffectual	Disdainful
Empathy	Envious	Helpless	Contemptuous
Awed	Enmity	Guilty	Antagonistic
Passionate	Disgusted	Worthless	Vengeful
Admired	Resentful	Important	Infuriated
Sympathetic	Bitter	Futile	Furious
Important	Detested	Distant	Aversion
Concerned	Fed up	At east	Cynical
Rejected	Alarmed	Abandoned	

Stepping Stones to a Healthy Stepfamily

www.janetnicholas.com